THAT MAN!

THAT MAN!

William & Nancie Carmichael

AND

Dr. Timothy Boyd

THOMAS NELSON PUBLISHERS
Nashville

Published in Nashville, Tennessee, by Thomas Nelson, Inc., and distributed in Canada by Lawson Falle, Ltd., Cambridge, Ontario.

Printed in the United States of America.

Unless otherwise noted, Scripture quotations are taken from THE NEW KING JAMES VERSION of the Bible. Copyright © 1979, 1980, 1982, Thomas Nelson, Inc., Publishers.

Scripture quotations noted NIV are from The Holy Bible: New International Version. Copyright © 1978 by the New York International Bible Society. Used by permission of Zondervan Publishers.

Scripture quotations noted NASB are from the New American Standard Bible, © The Lockman Foundation 1960, 1962, 1963, 1968, 1971, 1972, 1973, 1975, 1977, and are used by permission.

Library of Congress Cataloging-in-Publication Data

Carmichael, Bill.
    That man! / William and Nancie Carmichael, Timothy Boyd.
      p. cm.
    ISBN 0-8407-3070-5
    1. Men—United States. 2. Marriage—United States. 3. Sex differences (Psychology) 4. Interpersonal relations.
    I. Carmichael, Nancie. II. Boyd, Timothy. III. Title.
    HQ1090.3.C38   1988
    305.3—dc19   88-17458
                                                     CIP

1 2 3 4 5 6 — 92 91 90 89 88

To our children,
Jonathan, Eric, Christian,
Andrew, Amy, Sarah, and Cameron.

May they grow up
to be strong in God,
secure in themselves,
and happy in their
relationships.

CONTENTS

ACKNOWLEDGMENTS

This book, in order to address real people with everyday problems, contains portions of actual experiences with friends, subscribers, patients, and counselees. We have endeavored to preserve the confidentiality of those people. All case histories have been changed in regard to any information that could disturb that confidentiality. In fact, a number of the illustrations have been compiled from different cases in order to best demonstrate our point, while maintaining anonymity.

Our special thanks to the following people who have contributed to this book's success: Jerry Jones and Michelle Halseide, who did extensive and exhaustive research; Gayle Steely, who typed and retyped our ongoing changes in the manuscript; Brenda Rhyne, Tim's secretary, who helped to research and type his contributions; Craig and Eva Molan at Camp Davidson, who offered us gracious hospitality while we wrote this manuscript; and finally, to Tim's wife, Anita, for her patient love and steady support.

PART ONE

The Dilemma: We Are Different, We Are the Same

"You can't get any popcorn, Child. The machine is out of order. See, there is a sign on the machine."

But he didn't understand. After all, he had the desire, and he had the money, and he could see the popcorn in the machine. And yet somehow, somewhere, something was wrong because he couldn't get the popcorn.

The boy walked back with his mother, and he wanted to cry.

And Lord, I too felt like weeping, weeping for people who have become locked-in, jammed, broken machines filled with goodness that other people need and want and yet will never come to enjoy, because somehow, somewhere, something has gone wrong inside!

Andre Auw, "Out of Order"

CHAPTER ONE

PLAYING THE AGE-OLD GAME

He is playing masculine. She is playing feminine.
He is playing masculine because she is playing feminine.
She is playing feminine because he is playing masculine.
He is playing the kind of man that she thinks the kind of
     woman she is playing ought to admire.
She is playing the kind of woman that she thinks the kind
     of man he is playing ought to desire. . . .
So he plays harder. And she plays . . . softer. . . .
How do we call off the game?

Betty and Theodore Roszak, "Masculine/Feminine"

"We must think alike," Leslie told her mother. "Mark and I will be driving along the road somewhere and I'll bring up a subject out of the blue and he'll say, 'How strange you'd say that. I was just thinking the very same thing.' It's almost eerie. Do you think that means we were meant for each other, Mom?"

Leslie's mom is not so naive. Marilyn's been married long enough to know that a man and a woman can use the very same words without meaning the same thing.

"I wouldn't be so sure, Leslie," she replied. "There may be something to mental telepathy, but no way do you two think alike."

"Why do you say that? We both like country music and Chinese food. We read the same books and vote for the same candidates. We're both kind of shy and quiet. . . ."

"You're talking about personal tastes and personality types. That's not the issue," Marilyn argued. "I'm talking about more basic things like . . . ah . . . the way you set your priorities and the way you deal with your emotions, for instance. I'll wager you ten to one that Mark doesn't even think twice about staying at school for a holiday when he's got a term paper to do. You'd be home no matter what. I learned a long time ago that relationships mean much more to women, while tasks are top priority for men."

And so the debate goes on. Do men and women experience life differently?

Leslie's mother will have a difficult time getting her daughter to understand these differences now. Leslie is in love, and Mark is doing all the right things during this time of courtship.

For Leslie to understand that relationships inevitably change, she will have to experience life. How can she possibly know now that this man she has fallen in love with brings with him a whole laundry list of genetic and cultural "landmines"? They will begin to express themselves after marriage in ways that not only could alter the existing relationship, but could potentially damage or destroy it.

And for Mark, it is the same. He sees Leslie as a sweet, young, sexy woman, who has turned on every hormone in his body and has come into existence to fulfill his every need. To him, she is a prized possession. He has not yet learned that behind all this fragrance is an intricate and intelligent human being who will develop her own set of needs and goals and will eventually place some demands on him to help fulfill them. If Mark and Leslie's relationship continues to grow, they will have to face the age-old conflict that results from the biological, emotional, and social/cultural differences between men and women.

THE AGE-OLD CONFLICT

Hundreds of theories exist to explain why men and women are the way they are. While we are born distinctively male or female, it is also true that society teaches us how to behave. We are culturally conditioned into acting male or female. The God-designed, genetic givens of each individual interact with his or her life experiences and cultural influences. A complex maze of determinants is involved in the development of each person, and simplistic explanations such as "Men are men and women are women" are useless. That's why the apostle Paul believed that before we can obey Christ's radical teachings, we must be deprogrammed—transformed by the renewing of our minds so that we could be free from the cultural biases of our society.[1]

Since Adam ate the fruit, society has been busy telling men how to be men. Have you ever wondered, "Is this my imagination, or do men spend their lives performing—in sports, at sex, on the job—proving themselves in one way or another?" Two secular viewpoints on this subject—one written by a man, the other by a woman—demonstrate that even among professionals, our sex determines how we see this problem. Not surprisingly, both appear to be biased toward their own gender and tend to point the finger of blame toward the opposite gender.

A Man's Viewpoint

Dr. Warren Farrell, author of *Why Men Are the Way They Are*, traced a man's indoctrination to three stages, which, he said, have passed the "ring true" test in the more than three hundred men's groups with which he's worked.

In stage one, the prepubescent boy learns to desire a beautiful woman primarily by being exposed to suggestive advertising and television programming. Once in junior high, he quickly figures out that the most attractive girls are going out with older guys. Unless he stands out as a performer, he immediately feels inferior. So he does whatever it takes to earn the girls' attention, be it play football or become class president.

Farrell claimed that for decades marketing researchers have found that "the only common denominator that can appeal to men of all classes is their desire to achieve acceptance by the culture's most 'beautiful' women. Or conversely, the common denominator is their anxiety about being rejected by these women."[2]

In the process of learning how to perform, the young man discovers several things. First, all heroes are replaceable. Farrell wrote, "When a football player loses his position on the team, he seldom sees a cheerleader run off the field, saying, 'Wait, I'm still cheering for you—I love your openness and vulnerability.' He notices instead, that she cheers for his replaceable part . . . and so, even if he makes it as a hero in his field, he feels insecure."[3]

In addition, according to Farrell, he learns that it is not

popular to verbalize feelings, so he keeps them secret, even from himself. "He is learning, subconsciously, that *female support, nurturing, is conditional—it goes to the men on the playing field.* Therefore her *support* is really *pressure* to keep performing."[4]

This pressure is reinforced every day as he grows up with an increasing realization that a woman's love is conditional. He begins to sense that love may cost him. If he tells a woman that he loves her, he may get his fantasy, intimate contact. In return, however, he suspects that his "love" may mean a lifetime of mortgage payments.[5]

As puberty progresses, the boy learns that he has to be the initiator—the one who must risk rejection time and time again. Farrell poignantly wrote, "A boy learns he's supposed to want sex before he knows what it is, and now he learns he's supposed to initiate before he's even seen what he's reaching for."

During stage three the male's feeling of powerlessness makes his ego fragile and his self-concept vulnerable. And according to Farrell, vulnerability creates defenses. He cites three:

> *Defense 1:* The male turns women into sex objects because it hurts less to be rejected by an object than by a human being.

> *Defense 2:* He suppresses his sexual feelings and replaces them with dishonesty. Games work better than openness.

> *Defense 3:* The male resorts to "railroad sex." In other words, he refuses to prolong and master the friendship, believing that the longer he prolongs a friendship, the longer the period of potential rejection.[6]

Because this behavior turns off women, men become more desperately preoccupied with sex. (In a study conducted in 1978, Dr. Karen Shanor found that men between the ages of twelve and forty think of sex an average of six times per hour, every ten minutes.[7])

So how does the male overcome his feelings of powerlessness and vulnerability? He focuses all his efforts on the one thing that addresses every need and every defense: success. Success is his way of earning equality with women. It is his best defense against rejection. As Farrell concluded, "It is the male insurance policy."[8]

Let's look at an opposing theory, this one written by a woman.

A Woman's Viewpoint

Anne Wilson Schaef is a nationally known psychotherapist, lecturer, and writer, who helped found the Woman's Institute of Alternative Psychotherapy. In working with clients in her private practice, Schaef began to suspect that something was missing in the therapeutic process. After much research and years of interviewing women, she concluded that to understand what makes a person tick, you have to enter into the "system" in which that person lives. Schaef calls it the White Male System: "It is crucial to be able to define this system and deal with it simply because it surrounds us and permeates our lives. Its myths, beliefs, rituals, procedures, and outcomes affect everything we think, feel, and do."[9]

Schaef's theory is that societal norms have evolved in such a way that white males hold most of the power and influence in America. The White Male System makes our laws, runs the economy, sets our salaries, and decides when and if we go to war. She compares the system to pollution. If you live in a polluted city long enough, you start thinking that that's just the way air is. You don't realize that pollution is not natural until you get out of it. Many women are living in "polluted" environments, Schaef says, without realizing it. Thus, she contends that to survive in our culture, a woman must buy into the White Male System to some degree, which often means that a woman has to accept the stereotypes and myths it has set up for her. In *Women's Reality*, Schaef indentifies four myths that feed, sustain, and seek to justify the White Male System—myths that have been around so long most men are not even conscious of them and would probably deny their existence.

Myth #1. The White Male System is the only system that exists. Therefore, the beliefs and perceptions of other systems—especially any female system—are seen as stupid, illogical, irrational, crazy, or incompetent. Sure that the way they see the world is the way things are, men perceive any differences of opinion as threatening. All differences must be discounted, disparaged, or destroyed.[10]

Myth #2. The White Male System is innately superior. Note the breakdown in logic. If the White Male System is the only thing that exists, then how could it be superior and to what? Schaef says that most men aren't bothered by the inconsistency. She proposes that at some time they recognize that other systems exist, yet the White Male System represents reality and is therefore superior.[11]

Myth #3. The White Male System knows and understands everything. This is why women so frequently look to men for advice. Medical doctors, in particular, benefit from this tendency.

Myth #4. It is possible for a person to be logical, rational, and objective and thereby ignore his or her emotions or gut feelings. In support of this myth, many men spend a lot of time telling women that females are by nature not logical, rational, or objective.[12]

According to Schaef, to be born female in a culture permeated by the White Male System means that you are born "tainted." She acknowledges that men struggle with feelings of inferiority and low self-esteem, but she traces these feelings to a man's inability to be always superior.

When we discussed Schaef's theory of the White Male System with the women we interviewed, it nearly always struck a resonant chord. Most of the women we talked to said that her theory helped to explain the mindset of husbands, bosses, and subordinates. ("No wonder they are so stubborn and narrow-minded!")

Schaef goes on to say that women have developed several strategies to cope with their "assigned inferiority." Perhaps you've adopted one or more of these coping mechanisms. One of the most widely used strategies is to develop an incredible knack for remembering details of events, especially quarrels. Women's goal here is to prove themselves right about the facts of an issue or the circumstances of an event.[13]

Another strategy is "to overwhelm ourselves and those around us with our unquestionable goodness." Other women strive to be fair in all matters or to follow the rules so that they can become like everyone else and blend in. Still another strategy is to be understanding at all times because when a woman can *understand* why something happened, she can forgive.[14]

The Contrast

Note the rather glaring differences in the theories of these two professionals. Farrell (the man) claims that the pursuit of success produces characteristics in the male that do not always make him lovable at home or keep him alive for those he loves. Further, Farrell argues that men spend their entire lives attempting to achieve equality with women—not superiority.

Schaef, on the other hand, claims that her White Male System brings to light women's deep sense of having been "born inferior," a delusion stemming from a society that thinks men are superior.

The discrepancy between male and female authors demonstrates the divergent viewpoints. Men see life one way. Women see it another. Yet even with the obvious differences, both Farrell and Schaef come to strikingly similar conclusions.

Schaef concludes that coping strategies rarely work for the woman since they do not help her overcome her innate feelings of inferiority. So what does she do? *She takes her cues from society, which teaches her that once she attaches to a male, she can get validation and approval.* Then she will get over her feelings of worthlessness.[15]

Farrell comes to a similar conclusion. He argues that despite the women's movement, a woman's primary fantasy has not changed. This fantasy, he says, is of *marriage to one man who is able to provide security and options as to what she can devote herself to—work, home, children, or any combination thereof.* Her secondary fantasy is to receive excitement, respect, attention, romance, gentleness, and firmness from this same man. The problem, Farrell concludes, is that the man is too busy providing her primary fantasy to worry about her secondary one.[16]

Both theories really explain one thing—how a person acquires self-worth and a sense of security. A man seeks a woman; a woman seeks a man.

Differences do not have to mean conflict or competition. God intended harmonious relationships. In the end, we believe that men and women really do want the same essentials out of life.

HOW THIS BOOK BEGAN

We were aware of the conflicting viewpoints about the relationships between men and women. As co-publishers of *Virtue*, a Christian magazine for women, we wanted to know what kinds of problems our readers were experiencing in their relationships with men. What most frustrated them about men? Was it just obnoxious "male" habits, or did our readers' grievances run deeper?

Secretly, we also wanted answers for our own marriage. Were the growth pains we were experiencing unique to us, or were other couples' relationships stretching, changing, and at times in conflict? Were our differences just bad habits we needed to change, or did our male/female differences run much deeper?

We decided the subject would make a good feature article for *Virtue*. So we began by asking a random sample of five hundred *Virtue* readers about the relationships with the men in their lives—their husbands, bosses, fathers, brothers, sons, friends, and pastors. The response was overwhelming. Nearly 60 percent sent back the questionnaires, and most of them told us that yes, the relationships with men in their lives were, at times, both complicated and frustrating.

The random sample came from women who are traditionally motivated toward strong, healthy marriages and families. Here's a demographic profile of the women who responded: 85 percent, married; 65 percent, between the ages of 25 and 44, with an average of 2.3 children living at home; 94 percent had strong personal ties with a local church; 65 percent worked full or part time outside the home.

We expanded our inquiry to small discussion groups and individual counseling sessions. From the responses, we concluded that men share certain tendencies (just as women do) that cannot be explained by personality. At times they may be strengths, at other times weaknesses. Either way, the tendencies were often sources of hurt or frustration to many women. The men that most women pointed to as being a major source of frustration were their husbands followed by their bosses (a distant second), and their fathers (a distant third).

When asked, "Tell us what frustrates you or what you would most like to understand about your husband," one woman responded, "Why he can't tell me about what he's thinking or talk over deep feelings or problems with me." Another woman answered that she was frustrated by "his silence at times when I need to talk out problems in my life. He listens, but just doesn't understand."

To "What most frustrates you about men in general?" the following answer was typical: "Lack of understanding about a woman's feelings, and when you tell them how you feel, they either pooh-pooh it or forget about it, and nothing changes."

When asked what they would want if it were possible "to recreate men differently," women gave a common answer: "I would like him to be more able to understand my emotions and feelings. I would also like it if men could better tell you what they are thinking. I respect my husband more when he shows or shares emotions."

The theme that became quite evident was the seeming gulf in communication and intimacy between men and women.

The puzzling part was that these responses were not from women who had given up or were married to unreasonable tyrants. Most of the women we talked to were generally happy or at least still wanted the relationship with the man in their life to continue.

It was apparent that this chasm or gulf was perpetuated by a lack of understanding of each other's differences. As one woman aptly put it, "I'd like to know how men think and what makes them tick!" That thought seemed to be at the center of the frustration.

Somehow, we reasoned, if women could understand why

men are the way they are, maybe the hurts wouldn't be so painful, and maybe they could help the men in their lives "reprogram" the negative aspects of their male identities.

But by now, we both knew we were in over our heads in the effort to effectively deal with the problems we had uncovered and provide answers in a feature article. That's when we contacted Dr. Timothy Boyd, a good friend and a clinical psychologist with an active Christian counseling and treatment practice, and asked him to join us in our efforts to write a book to help women in their relationships with men.

Tim confirmed our findings by telling us that approximately 75 percent of his clients were women, many of whom consistently shared these same frustrations. Tim said, "My work as a psychologist puts me into contact on a daily basis with hurting women. Frequently, they will call for an appointment when they are in a crisis: their husband has decided to leave or they feel on the edge of a nervous breakdown. Often they will sit on the edge of the couch and plead with me for answers that will take away their pain."

Here's how one person expressed her pain:

> I feel frustrated and helpless. I don't know what to do. I'm tired of waiting for changes, searching for an effective approach, constantly being on guard, trying not to do or say anything that will create a bigger gap in John's and my relationship.
>
> I yearn to share John's life because I love him. I long to be his lover and his friend, his wife. I feel that I am just the person who takes care of his cooking, cleaning, and responsibilities while I watch him lead his own life. I don't share his life.

"I often find myself wishing I had a magic wand that could stop their hurting with just one wave," Tim said. "But I don't have any magic answers. Instead, I begin to try to help them understand the process of change. I say, 'Your problems did not spring up overnight. They are the result of years of experiences. Relationships that are splintering apart usually do not do so because of one trauma, but rather because of the accumulation of a thousand small wounds.'

"So I tell them that we have to lay a foundation. Some women get out the pick and shovel; some don't. The ones who do are the ones who see long-lasting, in-depth changes in their lives and relationships. Relief comes in time, but not immediately."

WHERE THIS BOOK WILL TAKE YOU

Our research showed us that a great number of women have not reached the point of no return but are emotionally dying in their relationships. One woman declared it this way: "Our relationship is emotionally sterile." Some women have labeled their pain, but many haven't. They know something very important is missing but are not able to understand what.

As you start to read this book, you may be in a lot of pain, perhaps in a relationship with a man that feels like a trap. As we go through these early chapters you may find yourself chomping at the bit, wanting to get down to the practical suggestions for making your life different.

After he had written some of the early material for the book, Tim said, "I asked my wife, Anita, to read it and give me feedback. Her response was, 'How does it apply to my life?' I found myself telling her then, as I am telling you, the reader, please be patient—we will get there!"

What we are trying to do first is to help you understand why things are the way they are between men and women. That knowledge will be like a map; it doesn't get you there, but it is vital to know the terrain. Reading the first part of this book is a necessary part of understanding how to change the relationships with the men in your life.

DIFFERENCE IS A BIOLOGICAL FACT

Unfortunately, our egalitarian society has confused equality with sameness. In the name of equal opportunity we have tried to obliterate the differences between sexes and cultures. In doing so, we have lost sight of the uniqueness of each. And often, we have taken away the very mark of individuality that is the core of a man or woman's self-esteem.

Difference is a biological fact. Equality is a political, ethical, and social concept. As sociologist Alice Rossi put it, "No rule of nature or of social organization says that the sexes have to be the same or do the same things in order to be social, political, and economic equals."[17]

Ironically, while trying to obliterate differences, our fallen society is equally busy teaching its youth that male and female are opposite sexes—polar opposites. For instance, man is strong; woman is weak.

We intend to challenge both tendencies. On the one hand, we seek to uphold God's original creation design—mutuality in equality, not male rulership over females.

On the other hand, we will argue that genetically and psychologically men and women are not the same and that if we can understand our differences, God-ordained and society-imposed, and learn to use them creatively, all of us, men and women alike, will be happier with ourselves and with each other.

One of the primary questions we will address in this book is, What is it about the male gender—the make-up of a man—that makes living, working, or communicating with him a different experience from doing the same things with female counterparts? Its corollary will take our inquiry one step further by asking, How can I adjust my attitudes, behavior, and leadership style to maximize the enjoyment or benefits of my relationships with men?

This book is not a glib attempt to tell you how to please your mates. This book is our response to a growing desire we perceive among women like you who want to find out what they can do to mitigate tension and develop healthy relationships that conform with the standard Christ enjoined us to uphold.

This is not to say that we should abandon the fight against sexual discrimination in the world and in the church. Rather, we are encouraging you to enlarge your focus to include a celebration of God-ordained differences between the sexes and begin to look for positive, active ways in which you can resolve conflict and assume complementary roles that demonstrate God's intentions for male/female relations. Our premise is that changing the men in your life is not your objective; understanding them is.

If you are like us, you are ready to face up to the painful

reality—that in our relationships we may have made some mistakes. But, as children of God, we can help transform our mistakes into miracles.

Once we develop an informed picture of the way men and women "tick," we can drop our idealizations and our expectations. If we can see each other more clearly, we can meet each other's needs more effectively and be less disappointed when another person acts differently from how we expected. The result is less anger and frustration.

True, there are risks involved in the process of building or rebuilding our relationships, just as there are risks in any relationship. "Will these changes work?" "Will he still love me if I make radical changes in how I relate to him?" "Is it worth the effort?" These are the risks you take. But we are convinced that the effort is worth the risks, and in the end the risks can have a positive effect. If you're at the point in your life when male/female relationships are no longer a source of anger, stress, hurt, confusion, or frustration, then this book has nothing to say to you—except, perhaps, to show you *why* your coping strategies got you through.

Hopefully, after reading this book you will not only have new insights into the men in your life, but new insights into yourself. And from these insights you will be able to develop a course of action that will move your life in harmony with God and your environment.

One woman we surveyed expressed our goal for this book when she said, "I want to have a greater appreciation of our differences and how we can use them to help each other to a better life. Besides, wouldn't it be boring if everyone were just alike and every relationship were identical?"

CHAPTER TWO

UNDERSTANDING THE DIFFERENCES

*N*o one can deny that anatomically a man's body is quite different from a woman's. Some of the differences are obvious; some are not. The growing trend in our society, however, has been to de-emphasize the biological differences between the sexes. In the name of equality, women are viewed as being able to perform the same tasks as men. Women now march along with men in the service ranks of our nation, and women are doing jobs that were once designated "men only."

In a recent court case in Oregon, a teenage girl and her parents brought suit against a school district because the girl was not permitted to wrestle on her high school team. The girl and her parents won the case. Some ask, "Why would a girl or her parents even want the girl to be on an all-boys wrestling team?" but others applaud the victory, viewing it as a blow against discrimination.

As a rationale for male domination, women have often been described as the weaker sex. After all, men are stronger than women and, therefore, better suited to take control. We intend to challenge the notion that men are *simply* stronger than women. It is not a simple matter. As we explore the intricacies of the biological differences between the sexes, we will see that men and women are *different* (not simply stronger or weaker). In some ways men are stronger than women, and in other ways women are stronger than men. Women can't run as fast or lift as much weight as men, but women's longevity is well established. As we understand more about the differences, it will become apparent that men and women really need each other. We can celebrate the differences once we understand them. Then we will be able to more rationally discuss how we will live, and we will be able to function more flexibly.

A missionary to Africa related a story about an American visitor to Zimbabwe. After observing the African women traveling a few paces behind their husbands as they walked down the jungle path, the visitor asked one of the women, "Why do you let him walk in front of you that way?" The surprised African woman replied, "But who would kill the snakes?"

As we begin to appreciate our biological heritage, some of the differences in the ways that men and women behave will become more understandable. And we can better deal with what we understand.

BIOLOGICAL DIFFERENCES

Let's look at how a fetus develops so that we understand how fragile our sexual identity really is. Every cell in our body contains forty-six chromosomes, each of them packed with genes in a mixture that's different for everyone. Out of the forty-six, two determine sex. They are called X and Y. Men have one of each, an X and a Y. The Y chromosome determines maleness. Women do not have a Y; they have two X's instead.

Every egg contains twenty-three chromosomes, one of which is an X. Every sperm also contains twenty-three chromosomes; but some contain an X, and others contain a Y. If an X-sperm fertilizes the egg, the embryo will have two X chromosomes, and the baby will be a female. If a Y does the job, an XY combination will produce a male baby.

In the first month or so after fertilization, the cells of the embryo divide and redivide until the fetus has a head and a body with arms and legs, but it is neither male nor female. About six weeks after conception, the fetus's sex is established. If nothing happens, the embryo's gonads will become ovaries. But if a Y chromosome is present and prodded into action, the fetus will develop testes.

Only in the last ten years have scientists discovered that a scrap of material called the H-Y antigen, which clings to the outside of male cells, must spur the Y chromosome into causing the embryo to develop testes.

But even then the baby's sex is not certain. Something else must take place. The hypothalamus, a part of the brain that governs such impulses as anger, hunger, and sex drive, must release a substance that tells the testes that it's time to start producing sex hormones.

Once in action, the testes put out a large amount of testosterone, the male hormone, and smaller amounts of estrogen and progesterone, the female hormones. This hormonal blend facilitates the further development of the sex organs.[1]

The point of this brief biology lesson is that from the beginning a man's sexuality is touch and go. Even a male fetus will become a healthy female if for some reason the gonads do not secrete sufficient testosterone while the fetus is in the womb.

A man's life also seems to be more fragile than a woman's. Dr. John Money and Dr. Stephen Wachtel, scientists who have studied fetal development, have determined that during the prenatal period there are 130 males for every 100 females. At birth, however, there are only 105 males for every 100 females. The gap lessens each successive year, until women outnumber men. Men die, on the average, eight years earlier than women. And of the fifteen leading causes of death, more men than women die from fourteen of them. Women are actually immune to some of the diseases that afflict men.[2]

Dr. Joan Ullyot, from the San Francisco Institute of Health Research, said, "Shipwrecked women survive better than shipwrecked men. It has something to do with better insulation or better natural ability to metabolize fat."[3] Dr. Estelle Ramey, an endocrinologist at Georgetown Medical School, stated that female astronauts could take "a lot more tumbling and disorientation than males without showing signs of shock."[4]

Given the early vulnerability of men, it seems likely that there is a corresponding insecurity. This could help to explain men's insistence that they are not weak, because we usually try to cover up our insecurities.

HORMONAL DIFFERENCES

There are some important differences between hormone production in the male and female bodies. The role of hormones in general, and sexual hormones in particular, is only now beginning to be fully appreciated. Scientists are finding more hormones (180 since 1970), and new information is accumulating so fast that textbooks can't keep up. "Everything is kept in perfect balance by hormones," says Dr. Bert O'Malley, chair of Cell Biology at Baylor College of Medicine, "not only for normal maintenance and survival but in response to anything that comes along—physical insult, mental stress, physical exertion, a thought process."[5]

One woman in our survey wondered, "Why do men always seem to put competition into so many situations?" Testosterone is a major factor.

Testosterone does several things in a man's body. It increases the tendency toward aggression and physical activity, and it spurs the sex drive and the ability to act on it. Have you ever wondered why little boys seem to delight in rough-and-tumble play and are fascinated with guns?

Tim tried to change this biological tendency but found out, as we all do, that sometimes our natural make-up is difficult to change. "My wife, Anita, and I consciously decided early in our parenting that we did not want our children to play with guns, so we never had any around the house and closely monitored other influences," Tim remembered. "This was certainly no problem for Sarah, who never seemed the least bit interested in guns. Much to our chagrin, however, Cameron, a loving and gentle child, had an ingenious determination to make a gun out of any material he could get his hands on."

We can conclude that sexual hormones do indeed affect that way we live and how we die. "Men were designed for short, nasty, brutal lives," said Dr. Ramey. "Women are designed for long, miserable ones."[6]

As a result of this built-in biological clock, men seem to develop a fatalistic view of life, which might explain why men are more prone than women to midlife crisis. They attempt to "grab all the gusto" before the candles they are burning at both ends go out.

SEXUAL DIFFERENCES

Aside from the obvious biological differences in the sexual organs of men and women, sexual differences take on profound cultural overlays. It's probably no secret to you that men and women often approach sex differently. Men, consistent with their performance orientation, focus on the physical aspects of sex, thus successful orgasm becomes the goal. Women are much more interested in the full expression of closeness and communication.

In studies by psychiatrist Marc Hollender, he discovered that some women trade sex (consciously or unconsciously) for being touched, held, and stroked. Their aim is not sex—it is to be close to another person.[7]

One woman in our study wrote, "I'd like to understand why my husband can't be satisfied with just some cuddling in between times of actual intercourse."

Helen Block Lewis, in *Psychic War in Men and Women*, stated that, "A man's failure to have an erection or to maintain it prevents intercourse; no such burden of responsibility for intercourse is carried by women. A woman has only to be there and willing to permit penetration. A man must be aroused—a state which is not necessarily under his conscious control. The act of intercourse is thus 'easier' for women, and her orgasm plays no role in her fertilization." This leads to feelings of fear for men that they will not be able to perform.[8]

Walter Trobisch, in *The Misunderstood Man*, expressed the idea that men do not feel "at one" with themselves sexually. His belief is that a man has a "peculiar and complicated relationship" with his penis. He wrote: "In contrast to the woman who feels at one with her sexual organs—they are a part of her—the man stands opposite his, as if it were another person, a stranger. The woman *is* her organ. The man *has* his."[9]

In the sexual relationship, men must continue to prove their manhood to women, but women, even if they are frigid, can have intercourse, become pregnant, and give birth. Women perform by merely *being*, without *doing*, while men must do something to be fulfilled. Sexual differences between men and women obviously contribute to our unique perspectives on life, and other anatomical differences increase this gap.

ANATOMICAL DIFFERENCES

Female sprinters cannot beat male sprinters. The reason? A male's larger bones are arranged differently. His shoulders are broader; his pelvis is more narrow. When he walks or runs, no motion is wasted. The female, by contrast, was designed for childbearing. Her larger pelvis causes her hips to sway as she moves, an attractive feature to men perhaps, but nonetheless a waste of motion for a sprinter.[10] What often happens is that this biological trait takes on a cultural overlay. Men often view the sway of a woman's hips as a deliberate attempt to be seductive. The "female" walk then becomes exaggerated, due to the response that it brings.

Have you ever wondered why men are usually better climbers, even on ladders? The reason is that the angle at which a woman's thigh is joined to her knee makes climbing more awkward.[11] Next time your husband laughs at your hesitancy to "scale the heights," let him know that there is a biological reason.

Although it doesn't seem fair, men can also lose weight more easily than women. A male's body contains a higher proportion of muscle to fat (muscle comprises about 41 percent of his body versus 35 percent of a woman's body), and muscle burns up five more calories per pound than fat does, just to maintain itself. In other words, the male metabolic rate is higher than the female's.[12]

One woman was frustrated when she and her husband decided to go on a diet together. His weight loss was more rapid than hers, on identical menus, so he accused her of fudging. If she had known about the physiological differences, she'd have had a quick answer to his accusation.

Basic differences in the ways that men and women use energy directly affect our behavior. A man's blood contains 20 percent more red corpuscles than a woman's. These cells contain hemoglobin, the substance that delivers oxygen to the body's billions of cells, and this oxygen works to release energy in fats and carbohydrates stored in the body. The more corpuscles the blood contains, the more oxygen the body gets and the more energy it has. That's why men typically have more start-up energy than women.[13]

On the other hand, it has also been discovered that women have greater endurance than men. Women's capacity for exercise drops 2 percent for each ten years of age, but the male capacity drops 10 percent for the same time period.[14]

Take two long-distance runners, for example. The male runner uses up his reserves of glycogen (the form in which carbohydrates are stored in the muscles) in about two hours if he's going at 80 percent of his capacity. At this point, he hits the wall, as runners say. By contrast, when a woman hits the wall, she can more easily keep going for a while because her body switches to its fat reserves. Pound for pound, fat yields twice as much energy as glycogen. And thanks to her sex hormones, the female's muscles easily use fat.[15]

This difference in the use of energy explains why a man is often fatigued after his work day and collapses in the lounger in front of the television, while his wife is still producing. The men hit the end of their reserves (just like the runner who hits the wall) while the women have reserves to draw on.

Biological, anatomical, and, finally, neurological differences between men and women contribute to our lack of understanding of one another.

NEUROLOGICAL DIFFERENCES

One woman in our survey admitted, "I don't understand a man's thinking process. Obviously they don't think the same way women do, and I often wonder what their thinking process entails." This woman was searching to understand the basic difference between the male and female brains, a difference which influences the way men and women think.

The fetus has what scientists call a "bipotential and undifferentiated" brain, which means it can go either way (male or female) depending on the influence of sex hormones. The brain is divided into left and right hemispheres. The left hemisphere (the verbal brain) controls language and reading skills. We use it when we "balance our checkbook, read a newspaper, sing a song, play bridge, write a letter. . . ."[16] The right hemisphere (intuitive brain) is the center of our spatial abilities. We use it when we "consult a road map, thread our way through a maze, work a jigsaw puzzle, design a house, plan a garden. . . ."[17]

Sexual differences in the way the brain is organized suggest different ways of thinking and learning. The male brain is specialized. A man uses one side for solving spatial problems, the other side for defining a word or verbalizing a problem. The female brain is not so specialized for some functions such as defining words. In other words, a woman's right-brain and left-brain abilities are duplicated to some extent in each hemisphere, so her right and left hemispheres work together to solve problems.[18]

Have you ever noticed that women can better sense the difference between what people say (the strict meaning of the words they use) and what they mean? Because a woman can zero in on a problem using both hemispheres of her brain, she is able to pick up the nuances of a person's true feelings and can perceive subtleties that go right past a man. Men do not understand this intuitive ability and tend to distrust it. In fact, when a woman picks up on a subtle criticism and confronts the man, often the man may respond that she is being oversensitive. This does not allow us to predict an individual's mental capacity based on sex, but it does explain why it is commonly recognized that women are more perceptive about people than men are. And that is one quality that makes a woman's input in a business decision especially valuable.

Another interesting aspect of the left/right brain hemispheres is that men and women approach problem solving differently. Men approach a problem in an analytical way—they separate themselves from it and deal with it abstractly. Women do not distance themselves from the problem; instead, they personalize it and maintain a personal identification. One woman, describing this difference said, "I think differently than they do. I work on several thoughts at once; they think and only want to hear about one thing at a time."

There are many other physical differences between men and women, but we do not intend to belabor the point. Suffice it to say that our physical make-up is foundational to the way we act, and the differences spring from the creative will of the Master Designer, who has equipped us to fulfill unique roles. We can echo King David: "We are *fearfully and wonderfully made*."[19]

CHAPTER THREE

WHERE IT ALL BEGAN: IMPACT OF THE FALL

Man's rule over woman is not the imperative order of creation, but rather the element of disorder that disturbs the original peace of creation . . . it is a prediction not a prescription.

Helmut Thielicke, The Ethics of Sex

*V*era Stewart has been married to John for thirty-eight years. She has never been to a counselor before, though she has confided in a couple of her female friends at various times over the years. She has been reluctant to seek counsel from her pastor because her husband is on the church board. John has a very strong personality and dominates their relationship. He has always held that men were created by God to rule over women and make important decisions. The Stewarts almost never quarrel, and Vera finds meaningful communication impossible. Vera has reached a point of frustration about being dominated and now questions whether or not she even loves John. She is seriously thinking about leaving him.

The role of women in society and the church is the subject of a lot of discussion in Christian circles today. John, whose behavior has become such an affront to Vera, was taught the glories of submission—that women are never to question and at all times are to defer to "godly men"—by his pastor. Under no circumstances are women to assert themselves, his pastor contended, or take leadership positions in the church structure. When Vera shared her frustration with the pastor, he counseled her that it was her biblical responsibility to stay under her husband's authority.

It's no wonder that some Christian women have formed an alliance with the feminist movement of our day. Issues like submission and ordination for women are hotly debated. We have found that Christian women are confused by the strident, yet contradictory, voices they hear. When they go with the voices that tell them to take a passive-dependent role, as Vera has, they often feel stifled and angry. When they go with the voices that tell them to rebel, they often feel guilty. Perhaps you have been caught in this bind and have experienced the anger and/or the guilt.

Before we can discuss male/female relationships intelligently, we must recognize that some Bible commentators and pastors have misused Scripture to support their personal doctrines of male supremacy. This is not the place to explore specific fallacies in great detail. And we are not so naive as to believe that this discussion will end the debate. We do feel, however, that some discussion of God's *original plan* will be helpful.

GOD'S ORIGINAL PLAN

What did God have in mind when He created gender? To answer this question we have to look at His *original* design—His blueprint—illustrated in the book of Genesis. In returning to the account of creation and the lives of Adam and Eve before the Fall, we could find no statement by God that men were to *rule* over women. Gilbert Bilezikian argued this point convincingly in his book *Beyond Sex Roles: A Guide for the Study of Female Roles in the Bible*. He wrote: "The fact that no reference is made to authority roles between man and woman in a text otherwise permeated with the concept of hierarchical organization indicates that their relationship was one of mutuality in equality and that considerations of supremacy of one over the other were alien to it."[1]

Bilezikian's point was that Genesis 1 meticulously defined the hierarchy of order for the entire universe—from the stars in space to the fish in the sea. Yet nowhere prior to the Fall did Scripture indicate that such a hierarchy existed between Adam and Eve. Neither did the issue of maleness or femaleness ever connote a disparity of rank or function. In God's original creation dream, man and woman were joint tenants. Both were blessed and both were made managers of planet Earth.

Unfortunately, many Christians have neither thought through these issues nor studied Scripture carefully enough to assume an informed point of view. Take the use of the word *helper* found in Genesis 2:18, for example. Here God said, "It is not good that man should be alone, I will make him a helper comparable to him."

In American culture, the word *helper* connotes subordination. The five-year-old who's helping Dad mow the lawn is "Daddy's little helper." Perhaps you, like many other Christians, have assumed that Adam was the boss and Eve was his underling when, in fact, the Hebrew word for *helper* means "one who stands alongside." It is usually attributed to God when He rushed in to rescue the Children of Israel. If anything the word suggests that without Eve, Adam was in trouble!

A study of the expression "and they shall become one flesh" (Gen. 2:24) also reveals something about God's original intent. The term *one flesh* is applied exclusively to a couple. It describes mutual dependency in an equal relationship. By contrast, *one flesh* is never used to describe the relationship between you and your child, but reserved for the relationship between you and your husband.

We've heard some people try to argue that because Adam was created first, the man is higher in God's hierarchy. Following this logic, we would have to conclude that the lizard is higher than man because it was created on the fifth day and man didn't come on the scene until the sixth day. That's obviously not the case, given that God told Adam that he was to rule over every living creature (Gen. 1:28).

We should note, moreover, that the female gender was not an afterthought or the icing on the cake, so to speak. To the contrary, *woman* was a vital component of the original *man*. The New King James Version's rendering of Genesis 1:26 and Genesis 5:1–2 underscores this fact. In Genesis 1:26 God said, "Let Us make man in Our image, according to Our likeness; let *them* have dominion over the fish of the sea. . . ." Genesis 5:1–2 reads: "In the day that God created man, He made him in the likeness of God. He created them male and female, and blessed them and called them Mankind. . . ."

In both passages, man (Adam) was a "them," the image of God in two parts: male and female. Man or woman alone did not contain all the attributes of God's character. Both maleness and femaleness were necessary to make a complete being. Dr. Donald M. Joy echoed this argument in *Bonding: Relationships in the Image of God:* "I now conclude that the first Adam was both male and female, and that the Genesis 2 record is a way of telling how the female was differentiated out of the male. I hypothesize further that by separating out the female from the male, both were magnetically charged to draw them back to the original unity or wholeness."[2]

Whether or not you agree with Joy's conclusions, the Genesis record does imply that God split the original Adam to distribute the full spectrum of His image into parallel and complementary packages. The "splitting of Adam"—the creation of male and female—suggests further, that some aspects of God's character are best illustrated by the female and others find better representation in the male.

Sounds great, right? But it's a far cry from where we find ourselves today. What happened to louse things up? Two words: *The Fall*.

God warned Adam not to eat from the Tree of Knowledge: "The day that you eat of it you shall surely die" (Gen. 2:17). According to Bilezikian, "The intrusion of death in the midst of life caused devastating reversals in the relationship of humans with God, within their own social structure, their vocational lives and in the ecological realm."[3] That wonderful, harmonious relationship Adam and Eve had enjoyed with each other deteriorated immediately.

The damage did not end there, however. Before the Fall, both man and woman were subject to God alone who had authority over them. But as Genesis 3:16 tells us, God made an observation about what sin was going to do to relationships: "Your desire shall be for your husband,/And he shall rule over you."

What did that mean? We think God was saying that Eve would want to perpetuate the intimacy she had once enjoyed with Adam. She would yearn for the one-flesh and seek attachment at all costs. But her nostalgia and desire for mutuality would not be reciprocated by her husband. Perhaps that's why many of the women we talked to found that instead of their husband's meeting their desires and providing a mutually supportive and nurturing family environment, the men tended to want to be boss. Often women complained that their husband made major family decisions without their wifes' opinions or feelings being considered. One woman, when describing this tendency, said, "He holds a close, tight rein on me, like I'd go out of control if he weren't watching." Another woman asked, "Why do men need to be 'top dog' all the time?"

Yet it's interesting that only *after* the Fall does the name *Adam* become the term used to designate man alone. But more telling still, Adam's first act as a fallen man is to name his wife Eve, thus announcing his control over her, just as they had earlier "named" the rest of creation.[4]

This tendency toward control addresses a major source of conflict we discovered in countless marriages. Women often complain that men do not invest as much emotionally in a relationship as do women. Husbands, women say, are not apt to read books on marriage or initiate marriage counseling. One woman said, "It's hard for them to open up and share how they feel—to become vulnerable."

Adam also had to cope with a new master—the environment. Having dismissed the original plan of God (a garden providing him with all his needs) through his rebellion, Adam became subject to his secondary source, the earth from which he came. This subjection has taxed man's abilities to the limit. Man is now busy trying to control his environment. As Dr. Joy wrote, "He will trouble-shoot the universe and will be driven with the urge to fix it, to make it run correctly."[5] As a result, he sees his task as competing with emotional attachments. One woman in our research put it this way: "What's really important to men? A lot of times it seems feelings and people don't matter, only things, schedules, and goals."

Further, because of the Fall, men tend to confuse women with property, attempting to control them instead of living in partnership with them. If this is true, it explains why many marriage relationships begin with mutual respect and joint tenancy and quickly shift to a vertical, hierarchical deformity, as in the case of Ralph and Lauren Stockman.

When Ralph and Lauren were dating, they enjoyed making decisions together. Lauren was impressed by Ralph's respect: he never tried to force her to do what he wanted. After they were married, however, she became more and more frustrated as Ralph insisted that she take her proper place and allow him to "wear the pants in the family."

Once a couple is married, a woman often tends to give up her independence, attach to a man—even worship him—and lose her direct and clear attachment to God. She learns to get what she wants through manipulation, by withholding her affections at the appropriate times.

A man, on the other hand, tends to start thinking of a woman as just one more material possession—something over which he must sweat, labor, and even exert control. He learns to manipulate her with power.

Diligent study of God's Word shows us not only what we're up against in this fallen world, but also that the entrance of sin into the world and the socialization of humanity have stacked the odds against healthy male/female relationships. Let's look at some cultural differences, which further illustrate the differences between men and women.

CHAPTER FOUR

LEARNING TO BE A WOMAN— LEARNING TO BE A MAN

*H*ave you ever stopped to consider what messages you received from your parents about how you, as a woman or man, were expected to act? You may have grown up believing that there were just certain ways that were *right*. After all, many believe, "Men are men and women are women, and there are no two ways about it."

In Chapter 2 we looked at the biological differences between men and women. Now let's look at the cultural influences. For instance, consider some of the traditional messages our culture has communicated to men, which crystallize the masculine/feminine polarity.

Man is the breadwinner. A man should take care of his family. If he doesn't, then he doesn't deserve to be called a man. Never mind that his wife is working too.

Don't think; do. Real men react fast and skillfully to critical situations. If someone invades his space, insults his woman, or questions his bravery, a man has every right to retaliate without thinking either before or after the fact.

Masculinity is sacred. Any attack on his masculinity must be met with force. Woman is inferior, yet she makes a marvelous trophy.

Be in charge. Stay in charge. A man must act as though he has the power to control and direct everything. He avoids being under the control of another (especially a woman) and never shows a hint of helplessness.

Be knowledgeable about "male" things and demonstrably ignorant of "female" things. Tools, cars, and football, for instance, are male domains, which women cannot understand. A man must act as though he knows everything about everything—except when it comes to performing traditionally female tasks. Then he must play dumb and awkward.

Perform sexually under any conditions. A man's man is able to perform sexually at a moment's notice. His sexual drives are strong, which he must demonstrate, and his abilities are unquestionable.

Don't quit until you're carried off the field. A man's body is indestructible, so he should never acknowledge physical limits or complain of fatigue. Real men are oblivious to danger or threat.[1]

The assumptions behind these male/female polarities are what one writer calls "masculine imperatives." Martin Acker, a professor of counseling psychology at the University of Oregon, teaches a course on the psychology of men. He defines masculine role-playing as the "musts" that color our perceptions and direct our behavior without conscious consideration, and he gives the imperatives we mentioned above as examples.

We usually don't stop to think about these messages, but that doesn't mean that we don't absorb them.

SOCIALIZATION

Socialization is a fancy name psychologists use to describe the way society asserts and we absorb the messages about how we are to act. "Society" includes the primary shaping forces—our mothers and fathers—in addition to the myriad other voices that affect and mold us. Those voices include our family, our peers, our teachers, television, other adults, movies, the church.

Consider the influence of the written media on the development of sex roles. In one study, Professor Marcia Gutentag and her colleagues analyzed the predominant themes in men's magazines and in women's magazines. They found striking differences. The magazines for men focused on adventure, overcoming obstacles, and success. Women's magazines addressed issues of relating emotionally to others and how to handle loss (loss of relationships, of competency, of looks).[2] So as you read *Good Housekeeping* and your husband reads *Sports Illustrated*, you are both being shaped and influenced.

How do we know to what degree we are the product of our biology (which we examined in Chapter 2) and to what degree we are the product of our society? *There is a complex interaction between the two. They become quickly intertwined after we are born* so that we soon lose the connection between the two and thus have difficulty determining which is the predominant force.

The Intertwining

From the moment of birth, boys and girls relate to their environment differently. At first, this difference is probably biological. For instance, in a study of one hundred newborns (in which researchers were trying to find out if infants could differentiate between the sound of another child's crying and an artificial sound) it was discovered that girls were more responsive to the crying of other infants than boys were, and girls started crying along with other babies more readily than boys did. In addition, female infants "smiled" more (a reflexive smile). They also babbled more in response to the sight of a human face.[3] One fascinating study determined that female babies at the age of three months preferred photos of human faces, whereas the male babies showed no preferences.

These differences between newborn girls and boys indicate that even from the earliest age girls have a built-in predisposition toward being tuned in to others, which has an important effect on our relationships. In our survey we found that women were very frustrated with the men in their lives with regard to one issue: the men's emotional detachment from others. "He doesn't understand or relate to how much I love family members or friends," one woman said. "He lacks the compassion that I have for certain people. It's frustrating to the point he can't share the same joys or hurts I share with those people—even with God. We relate so differently."

This innate difference between male and female soon becomes intertwined with the influence of all the voices that assert their shaping influence on us. For example, from the child's birth, parents start sending cues of how to act as a male or a female. Girls are to wear pink, boys are to wear blue. There is nothing innately feminine about pink or masculine about blue, but we have assigned labels to those colors.

A study of parents' reactions to one-day-old infants revealed that sons were described as "big, tough, and active," and girls were seen as "little, beautiful, pretty, and cute." The descriptions had nothing to do with the actual appearance of the babies.[4] Have you ever seen a new father, beaming with pride because of his man-child, stick a football in the baby's crib? It's almost as if he's hoping that the "magical" presence of the masculine object will rub off on the boy and will ensure his development as a "real man." Mothers, too, will work their "magic" by dressing up their little girls in frilly, lacy garb.

One study examined the interactions between mothers and their infants and found that mothers tended to hold baby boys further away from their bodies than they did baby girls. They also held baby boys more often in a standing and sitting posture (requiring the child to support more of its own weight) and tended to stimulate their boy children more than they did girls. By the age of three months the baby boys were generally more fussy and irritable than the girls, who tended to sleep more and cry less than the boys. In addition, the mothers tended to give more attention to their infants when they were cuddly and less when they were fussy, thus the girls inevitably received more attention than the boys.[5]

Studies have shown that infant girls bond earlier with their mothers than do infant boys.[6] And girls are more upset by separations. A study of thirteen month olds revealed that girls were more reluctant to leave their mothers. When the researchers erected a net barrier and separated the children from their mothers, girls tended to stay near the center of the net, cry, and motion for their mothers. Boys were more prone to try to get around the end of the barrier, not waiting for someone else to resolve their dilemma.[7]

Here we can see the beginnings of patterns that later manifest themselves as distinctive traits of men and women. Boys are trained to be independent; girls are affirmed for being dependent. Boys get praise for taking risks and acting aggressively; girls are rewarded for compliance and for being cute and sweet. As a result, girls and boys demonstrate early differences in the way they relate to others.

Relating to Others

At a recent church gathering—while playing board games—
Tim found himself fascinated by the difference between the way
the men and the women spent the evening. The men tended to
pick a game, set it up, and get down to the business of competing: The central focus was the game. The women gradually
drifted into playing games, but the central focus was not the
game, but the exchange of information and the visit.

An interesting piece of research was conducted by Janet
Lever with regard to the differences in the sexes as related to the
games children play. She found that boys' games tended to last
longer because boys were able to resolve disputes more effectively
than girls. When a dispute came up, boys were more likely to
refer to the rules and deal with conflict in a straightforward,
competitive manner. In contrast, girls emphasized cooperation,
preferring to stop the game rather than fight it out. Girls tended
to be more pragmatic about the rules and could make exceptions
more easily. As adults, men still have a tendency to gravitate to
"black-and-white" thinking, whereas women are able to be more
flexible and to see things from others' points of view.[8]

The tendency for girls to center their energy on building
relationships while boys center theirs on achievement can be
seen in a child's early development. In a study of four thousand
children, aged ten to nineteen, the children were asked what
their biggest personal problem was. The girls viewed family and
interpersonal problems as being the most significant, yet the
boys chose achievement and financial problems.[9]

A study on socialization patterns showed that boys tended
to collect in small groups or gangs and compete. Girls tended to
enter in with one or two others and have intimate conversations.[10] Thus, at an early age, the pattern is set for adulthood.
Men play their softball and tell "war stories," while women coffee
klatch and share their personal joys and frustrations.

THE DEVELOPMENT OF MALE
SEXUAL IDENTITY

We asked the women in our survey this provocative question: "If God were to come to you and say that He is getting ready to re-create man, how would you suggest that man be created differently?" One comment was indicative of many women's feelings: "I would like the macho gene removed." Perhaps you can identify with this woman's frustration.

Studies have shown that males have great difficulty in developing a firm, nondefensive sexual identity because of the way in which boys are taught to be male. Whereas girls are able to look to their mothers for direct models of how to act as a girl, boys' fathers are often less available as models so boys must learn how to act through means other than direct imitation. The learning of the male identity occurs, then, as the boy learns to act *differently* from his mother. In essence, he has to "squash" the mother out of himself.

Carol Gilligan, in her book *In a Different Voice,* explained the future implications of this difference:

> Since masculinity is defined through separation while femininity is defined through attachment, male gender identity is threatened by intimacy while female gender identity is threatened by separation. Thus, males tend to have difficulty with relationships, while females tend to have problems with individuation.[11]

Most of us have observed boys as they are placed under early pressure to keep from acting feminine. Directions such as "Don't be a sissy," "Don't play with dolls," "Don't be a cry baby," are delivered with great emphasis. You will recall that we said earlier that the hormone testosterone is instrumental in the tendency for males to be more aggressive. This tendency is heightened, however, when parents not only tolerate but often promote aggression.

Footballs, toy guns, roughhousing are all seen as normal play patterns for boys. And fathers like their boys to appear masculine. Bill observed a father with two little boys in a frozen yogurt store. The boys were dressed just like their dad, with cowboy boots, hats, and western jackets—one of sheepskin, lined with red plaid; the other, a denim jacket exactly like his father's. The little guys even swaggered like their dad.

As he handed the yogurt cones to the dad, the clerk asked, "What are you up to today?"

"We're going out to terrorize the town," Dad replied in his best John Wayne voice. He punched the older son in the shoulder in an "Aren't we, buddy?" gesture.

As they turned toward the door, the younger son put his coat back on, thrusting his arm into the sleeve as if the coat were a punching bag. "Atta boy," the father said, encouraging the child's aggressiveness. This father was sending very clear, though unspoken, messages to his sons about the type of behavior he desired.

One of the important early expectations placed on boys is that they suppress their emotions. Bernie Zilbergeld, in *Male Sexuality*, stated that men

> learn early that only a narrow range of emotion is permitted . . . aggressiveness, competitiveness, anger, joviality, and other feelings associated with being in control. As we grow older sexual feelings are added to the list. Weakness, confusion, fear, vulnerability, tenderness, compassion and sensuality are allowed only to the girls and women. A boy who exhibits any such traits is likely to be made fun of and called a sissy or a girl (and what can be more devastating?).[12]

One woman's touching comment from our survey summed up many women's feelings regarding men's difficulty in expressing emotion: "Even after twenty-two years he keeps it all to himself. I would like him to share more of his feelings and know more of 'where he's coming from. . . .' Soul-baring would be a great experience for both of us."

Athletics often becomes the arena where boys show their skills and demonstrate that they are not sissies. When a boy is not skilled or interested in sports, he suffers the disapproval of his peers. Tim remembers the pressure he felt as a youth to act "like a man":

> I now remember, with a certain degree of amusement, a scene from my high-school gym class. Back then, however, it was a time of intense feelings of inadequacy. I didn't have anyone to teach me how to move my body in a coordinated,

athletic way (my father and I were emotionally distant and my older brother was already in college), and, in addition, my growth spurt had rendered me incapable of walking and chewing gum at the same time. We had one of those gym teachers who fit the stereotype: He cussed, chewed, and grunted a lot. He was also the football coach and had a special affinity with "his boys" (the team members), who didn't have to dress down for P.E. class and got automatic A's.

Periodically he conducted an exercise in public humiliation, which I grew to hate. We were expected to perform various tasks, such as doing the greatest number of pushups that we could in a certain time period. Not only did our grades depend on how many we could squeeze out, but we also had to publicly reveal how many we did. Tacked up on the gym walls were the names of the "immortals" who had given record-setting performances.

I was paired with another kid named Rocky Bowzer, who was going to count my pushups and I would count his. Rocky, who was not exactly Albert Einstein, *was* gifted with an Apollo-like body. In fact, he had already started to shave, and I didn't even know how a safety razor worked. Fortunately for me, however, Rocky was interested in getting into the record books, so we had an agreement. We were supposed to come all the way down to the floor with each pushup, but Rocky counted my "halfways" and I counted his. I was never so happy. Rather than feeling like a total wimp when it came time to shout out my total, I only felt like a partial wimp.

CHANGING ROLES (FOR BOTH MEN AND WOMEN)

One of the reasons *our* generation is more complex in this area of male/female roles and expectations is that we are a "transition" generation. That is, we are mixing older, more stabilized male/female roles with some rather new ideas, which emerged from the feminist movement.

As a result of these changing roles, people are often confused about what they should be doing and for whom. In many instances they've lost all sense of their unique contribution to their family and society. Their confusion and loss of identity lead to stress and conflict in relationships.

Today both men and women are receiving mixed messages about their expected roles: Be tough; be vulnerable. Be self-controlled; be open. Be independent; be tuned in.

As we've already pointed out, some socially imposed stereotypes (such as being "Mr. Macho") are harmful. But most men have seen *their* way of viewing masculinity as *sacred*, and anything considered sacred is slow to change. This is one reason so many men are holding to traditional masculine roles or expectations and resisting new ideas.

The unfortunate thing about our reliance on socially imposed sex-role expectations is that they can often limit our potential. When asked if he would like to be a ballet dancer, Tim's seven-year-old boy, Cameron, replied, "No way! I'm a boy." Sex-role stereotypes also set up dichotomies: Girls nurture; boys achieve. The resulting behavioral patterns may well mean that fathers leave the nurturing of children to mothers, and women leave the achieving to men. If men are not supposed to cry, their ability to express painful emotion is limited.

But are traditional male/female roles and expectations sacred? Are the traditional male traits described in this chapter the biblical model? Is this male/female role polarity God's design or cultural bias?

How much of our feeling that this is the way it is supposed to be is a result of our "being conformed to this world" instead of "transformed by the renewing of our minds"? We believe that our role prescriptions are often not God-designed, though they are often presented that way.

Our examination of the social factors in sex-role development has unearthed some clear patterns. We can see how, from the moment of birth, boys and girls are treated differently. Patterns develop and roles emerge. These patterns and roles give us structure for our lives; they give direction, goals, and cues for appropriate behavior. They also tend to restrict us and to stifle individuality. There are other unfortunate by-products of some of the sex-role stereotyping—feelings of inferiority, fear, and hostility for both men and women. We will examine these in the next chapter.

CHAPTER FIVE

THE INSECURITY TRAP

*B*y now you may be feeling like Debby, one of the women Tim counseled, felt. "Dealing with a man's ego is like walking on eggs," she complained. "I have to weigh what I say, how I say it, and when I say it. By the time I finish calculating, I'm too tired to say it!"

Although Debby understands the fragility of the male ego, like many women, she's tired of hearing about it. "I listen to all these talk shows and I can't tell you how many psychologists and psychiatrists talk about male insecurity. Frankly, I think it's a poor excuse for treating women like trash."

It does make you wonder, particularly when your boss criticizes your work and your husband criticizes your domestic skills. "What a joke," you may say. "My husband doesn't have an insecure bone in his body." That may be your perception based on the good front he puts up or on his attitude of superiority.[1]

In our survey we discovered that when asked "What frustrates you about men in general?" women frequently verbalized their feelings of being "put-down" by men. The following are some typical responses from women who were angry with and hostile toward the men who had given them "put-down" messages:

- "They expect women to pick up their slack and cover their tracks. They too often treat women as servants, even when the woman is equal in position. They *constantly* joke about women's foibles."
- "My husband will correct something I've done or step in and take over a situation as though I'm not capable."
- "They have an inability to recognize that a woman can at times, and with many things, do a better job than they can."

Ironically, women do often feel and act inferior to men. Yet

49

they are actually much more secure in their sexual identity than men are. Men, on the other hand, though feeling superior, have deep feelings of insecurity about their manhood. This may sound like a riddle or a paradox; nevertheless, it is true. Women feel inferior; men feel insecure. Let's discuss these two ironies and their impact on our relationships with the opposite sex.

FEMALE INFERIORITY

One study asked the question, "Are men or women superior in worth?" It may come as no surprise to you that men rated themselves superior to women. In another interesting study, men and women were given identical articles to evaluate signed by "John McKay" and "Joan McKay." Again, men rated the articles more highly if they thought the writer was male.[2]

It may surprise you, however, that both of these studies found that women tended to agree with the men: *The women put themselves down.* Have you ever noticed how women tend to devalue women? Perhaps you've caught yourself minimizing your own accomplishments or contributions to life. If so, you fit a typical pattern.

A study of girls' and boys' expectations of success showed that boys who were bright expected to perform well in the future, and they attributed their success to their own doing. In contrast, bright girls who did well on the tests attributed their success to reasons other than their own ability.[3]

These studies lead us to ask where these feelings of female inferiority come from. The answer is that we were not born with this prejudice: we learn it very early in life.

A fascinating study was carried out by Alice Baumgartner and others at the University of Colorado.[4] They asked two thousand children (grades three through twelve) the question, "If you woke up tomorrow and discovered you were a boy/girl, how would your life be different?" Generally, both girls and boys rejected the idea of being female (sometimes with contempt). Here's a sampling of some of their comments:

- Fourth-grade boy: "I wouldn't like having a little pink dress or anything about a girl. It wouldn't be fun."

- Sixth-grade boy: "If I were a girl, I'd be stupid and weak as a string."
- Fourth-grade girl: "If I were a boy, I would be treated better. I would get paid more and be able to do more things."
- Eleventh-grade girl: "People would take my decisions and beliefs more seriously."

The eleventh-grade girl could have been speaking of an incident that took place in Bill and Nancie's living room, which showed that no family is exempt from the development of this bias.

Bill sat down with his four sons to watch the Seattle Seahawks play football. To their surprise, the play-by-play announcer was a woman. The boys looked at Bill and each other in disbelief. Chris, age fifteen, turned to Bill and loudly exclaimed, "Gross!"

"What's gross?" Bill asked.

The others chimed in at that point and said, "A woman announcer—it just doesn't seem right."

Before Gayle, the female announcer, could start talking about "slot backs," "wide receivers," and "blitzes" (which, in Bill's opinion, she did a very good job) the boys were making comments like, "What does she know about football? She's never played the game." (Neither had any of them.) For most of the game the comments and attention kept focusing on Gayle instead of the game.

At one point one of the boys said, "How can Dave [the male color commentator working with Gayle] stand to work with her!"

The startling discovery is that boys learn early in life to devalue women, and girls learn just as early to devalue themselves. Thus, the pattern is established, and as males grow older, they become increasingly established in the superiority of the masculine role. By the end of their first year of high school, boys feel much more positively about being boys than girls feel about being girls. In addition, males' ego strength increases whereas girls' ego strength declines. As men become more firmly established in the male role, they increasingly reject the female role.

MALE INSECURITY

In light of the male's feeling of superiority, it may seem il-logical to you that men feel insecure. Nevertheless, many men do feel insecure. Every man wears his insecurity differently: Some even disguise it as "pride." (It sounds better to say that so-and-so has a lot of pride than it does to label him as insecure.) And some men are more prone to feelings of insecurity than others.

However, if you can put prejudices aside, you might find that the idea of male insecurity explains quite a bit about the men in your life. Just keep in mind that how you *think* your part-ner feels may not be how he *really* feels. If you can accept that your perceptions may be inaccurate to some degree, you can come away with some helpful insights.

One woman from our survey wondered why her boss used a "cheery, carefree attitude to cover up for his incompetence and self-doubt." Chances are her boss, if asked, would have vehe-mently denied any feelings of insecurity. If she confronted him directly, he might have even become defensive and accused her of being the one with the problem.

Often the hostility men express toward women (with its more subtle variations of indifference and devaluation) is actually the fear of men.[5] Afraid of their feelings of dependency on women and their underlying wish for a mother's protection, they become counterdependent. In *The Misunderstood Man*, Walter Trobisch claimed that the typical male dreams of himself as the Great Lover—the one who gives in a relationship—when, in fact, he senses deep within that he has been on the receiving end since the beginning of his life—and it is the woman who is the giver. After all, his mother "gave" him birth, his wife "gives" him her body.[6]

Many men look at their wives as replacements for their mothers. One of the most common complaints that Tim hears from married women who come in for counseling is, "I wish he would grow up and stop expecting me to treat him like his mother does. I already have two kids, but I feel like I have three." Wives frequently become their husband's support system, since they maintain the home base where the husband refuels before he goes out into the "jungle" for another day. Wives listen to their husband's problems, bolster them up, and try to keep things smoothed over. It is no wonder that statistics have shown that when a man's wife dies, he has a good chance of getting seriously ill within the first year after her death. Women who lose their mates are much less prone to the same response.

Men are unsure how to let themselves need a woman. It arouses many feelings that they are uncomfortable with when they allow themselves to feel. Feeling needy can be a strange and fearful experience when you have been avoiding the feeling for years. Many men feel more comfortable having the woman assume the passive role, letting her be the needy one. This means a denial of certain longings, but it seems the safest.

Men may work hard to keep their wife in the needy position, but if they do they actually put themselves in a bind. When their wife comes to them with her requests for emotional support, men feel inadequate to meet those needs. As Trobisch put it, "It's as if something deep within her is always crying for comfort, and it dawns on him that he will never be able to satisfy completely her deepest longings. . . . So all too often he resigns, he gives up the struggle and takes refuge among other men—in his factory, with his recreational hobbies, at the office. . . ."[7]

The men who unconsciously choose passive women as their mates and keep them under their thumbs often display typical macho behavior and make a point of avoiding anything that could be interpreted as weakness. Under the "in-control" exterior, however, lurks a great deal of insecurity. Afraid to develop a relationship of equality with their wife, these men ensure their emotional safety by maintaining control.

Men end up in what behavioral psychologists call an "approach-avoidance" conflict. It's like the rat who wants the food in the dish on the other side of his cage but is afraid of getting an electrical shock if he steps over a certain line. Men desire closeness to and *even dependency* on women, but they fear the pain of getting hurt and the "loss" of their masculinity. (Remember: Only weak men are ever dependent!)

Men appear, at times, to be afraid that they might revert to acting female. Thus they often develop subtle (or overt) hostility against women and attempt to dominate them. Men will cover up their soft interior and cut themselves off from tender feelings.

The result is unfortunate: Men put their energy into being strong and rational and successful, and they neglect their emotional life. Their inner life becomes barren, but they are so invested in future goals that they can be out of touch with what is missing.

Have you ever wondered why women seem to be much more oriented toward developing their spiritual lives than men? Many men fear closeness with God, just as they fear closeness with their wife, because it means being dependent. In our survey we found that many women not only knew men with this tendency but were frustrated by their failure to follow God or even to strive to know Him.

THE EFFECT OF THESE IRONIES
ON YOU AND ME

It is no secret that our Western culture is essentially masculine; it is a society of things. Power, reason, and technology are the primary orientation—not relationships. Historically in America, feminine values have become devalued. Function validates the person, not vice versa.

As our society has placed a high value on achievement and the acquisition of material goods, both men and women have come to look at housework as unimportant. Thus women who spend much of their time in this activity can end up feeling unappreciated. This devaluation does nothing to help them feel positive about their tasks.

Women judge themselves in terms of their ability to be caretakers. Men, however, emphasize individual achievement, so they tend to devalue the "caretaker" role. When men act aggressively, they feel strong. In contrast, women feel strong when they act lovingly.

Girls learn early to empathize, to experience the needs and feelings of another as their own. Rather than viewing this as a strength, men often view women's empathic, or intuitive, abilities as a weakness and see them as being overemotional. When threatened by emotion, men try to shut it down. Thus, discouraged by male derision, women will put themselves down for being "too emotional," when in fact, their emotionality is a gift of God.

By being appealing and understanding, by giving pleasure to another, women hope to get their needs met. Therefore, they respond to the attitudes and feelings of others. To women, interpersonal interactions are ends in themselves. To men, relationships are means to an end. For women, loss of a key relationship is not just the loss of a relationship; it comes closer to being the loss of part of themselves. Men do not usually experience loss this way.

Men, with their usual insistence on independence, are able to keep themselves emotionally safe. Women, in contrast, are more vulnerable because they open themselves up to and long for closeness with men. It's as if a woman stands on the outside, banging on the door, crying out to be let into her husband's inner world. She wants love and friendship. The man, in contrast, feels as if he is being assaulted and keeps the door bolted.[8] In the resulting stand-off neither the man nor the woman feels fulfilled.

Have you ever noticed that men will talk about facts and ideas and feel as if they are fully communicating? Even when men do try to express their emotions, they often lack the necessary skills. They become confused and frustrated when their partners want more.

Men have been pushed to develop their outer selves (to achieve success); women have been encouraged to develop their inner selves.

Although a man may not outwardly act this way, his greatest fear is that if he exposes his weaknesses, allowing a woman to see him as he really is, she will no longer love him. Fear of rejection, then, becomes a formidable barrier to his honest sharing of feelings. Because a man is afraid of being hurt through rejection, he retreats or counterattacks.

Often this counterattack strategy consists of the male's asserting his superiority and right of control over others, especially women. He declares his wife to be his private possession. If he is a Christian, he often clings to verses such as Ephesians 5:24, which, taken out of context, suggest that his rightful duty is to rule over his wife with an iron fist.

What is the solution? First, it is important that you remember that your feelings of inferiority and the man in your life's feelings of inadequacy are not part of God's original design. Second, if you allow yourself to be transformed through God's power and guidance, you can shed your inferior feelings. As you understand men's insecurity, you can help them to accept who they are. Third, remember that each of you has qualities that are greatly needed by the other. As Matteson stated in *Adolescence Today*:

> The strength we identify with masculinity is of positive value, except when it loses touch with the personal. The emotionality and warmth of femininity is corrupt only when it is restricted and thus becomes possessive and turns relationships into closed, stagnant systems. Too many of our youth have become depersonalized men and resentful women.[9]

CHAPTER SIX

WHAT MOTIVATES A MAN?

"*T*he honeymoon must be over," Shelly snapped at her husband. Just home from work, Craig had whisked past her on his way to the refrigerator. "What happened to 'Hello beautiful, I missed you today'?"

Craig rolled his eyes and laughed. "Sorry, honey. I'm just beat, that's all." He gave her a halfhearted hug and headed toward the TV.

"I hate to bug you about this, Craig, but I feel taken for granted. I rush home to freshen up and fix a nice dinner for you, and all you can do is mumble 'Hi.'"

"I said I was sorry. What do you expect?" he retorted.

"A little attention, that's all!"

And so the tug of war goes on. What Shelly doesn't realize is that, for Craig, the most important part of his day—earning a living—ended when he walked through the front door. To Craig, home is the place where a man recharges his batteries.

For Shelly, however, the most crucial part of the day—making a connection in a relationship—is still to come. At home Craig wants to tune out; Shelly wants to tune in. Beyond her own needs for privacy, Shelly desires emotional contact with her husband.

Does this scenario sound familiar? It is this kind of situation that leads many women to conclude that men are task oriented, not relationship oriented. And, for the most part, that assumption is correct. For Nancie, this point was vividly demonstrated one Christmas:

> Bill has spoiled me with his creative and lavish gifts. One year it was two tickets to Hawaii. Once it was a coat. He's given beautiful lingerie, perfume, or sports outfits. Bill's gifts spell "fun-sweetheart-girlfriend." *Never* an appli-

ance, food processor, or vacuum, for which I have been secretly and endlessly grateful. It doesn't matter that those other kinds of gifts would be more useful or needed!

But last Christmas we were pinching pennies. We faithfully promised each other we would hold to a strict budget—which I held to by getting a great buy on a jacket for Bill. Sure, Christmas is for kids, but I could hardly wait to see what my dream man would get me.

I opened the gift in amazement. There, still factory-wrapped in cellophane, were a full-sized Roget's Thesaurus and a Webster's dictionary. Bill watched me, beaming. ". . . I heard you say you needed those for your office," he was saying. My heart fell.

He was right. And we were involved in book projects. Yes, I needed them. What a good idea. I forced a grin. "Thanks, honey. Just what I needed!" Inside I was devastated. What did he think I was—a prudish librarian? What could you write in the flyleaf of a dictionary to your sweetheart? "Darling, I haven't the words to describe how much you mean to me. . ."

Later we laughed about it when we realized it was part of our natures to view these gifts so differently. Bill saw the books as tools that would be used. I was looking for something that would speak of relationship. Even a book of poetry would speak of romance. A dictionary and thesaurus, albeit incredibly useful, seemed at that time to me to be impersonal. (I must confess, they have been two of the best and most-used gifts Bill has ever given me. I just can't wear them!)

Even the kind of gifts we give (i.e., practical vs. intimate), reinforce the task-oriented/relationship-oriented difference between men and women.

MALE MOTIVATIONS

If you think back to Chapter 1, you will recall that both Warren Farrell and Anne Wilson Schaef also made comments revealing their belief that, for the most part, men are task oriented rather than relationship oriented. And we pointed out in Chapter 3 that this tendency began with Adam after the Fall. As

Donald Joy put it, "He will trouble-shoot the universe and will be driven with the urge to fix it, to make it run correctly."[1] In Chapter 5 and in this chapter, we've documented that men have been enculturated into this task-oriented behavioral pattern for centuries.

Men's task orientation colors their relationships so their relationships with others become tasks to be accomplished instead of living, dynamic bonds to be nurtured. Anne Wilson Schaef described this phenomenon in *Women's Reality:*

> I used to think that men moved into the Female System during courtship. At that time, a man seems to set aside his self and his work and put the relationship at the center of his universe . . . . As soon as the relationship is "nailed down," however—as soon as the man is sure of the woman's affections, and they are either married or have settled into some other committed arrangement—he goes back to his self and his work.[2]

But now, having discussed this tendency with many men, Schaef believes that men make no such move into the woman's world. What she hears them saying is this: "The relationship is a task (work) to be accomplished, and when it is solidified and we are sure of it, we go back to our self and our work and business as usual."[3]

Interestingly, the very same thing frequently happens during a marriage crisis. In Tim's experience, the woman is often the first one to seek a marriage counselor in a breakup. The man waits until the last minute or after it's too late. As Tim says, if the wife has left the husband, he becomes desperate. Frantic phone calls from the man wanting an appointment in the next thirty minutes are typical. All too often the husband will say, "Tell me what I need to do to get her back." In other words, restoring the marriage becomes a new task: "I won her once. What do I need to do to win her again?" Even in this crisis he is task oriented rather than relationship oriented.

In fact, this task orientation (i.e., doing rather than being) is so strong with most men that it becomes the foundation for their commitment. Right or wrong, a man views marriage as not only a commitment to be faithful but also an alliance of obligation. The subtle messages he receives from his wife, perhaps, and certainly from the world around him, tell him that to keep his wife's interest he must provide her with financial security and status. Success at work and being loved by a woman are inseparable to him. So he sees "work as usual" as an important contribution to the relationship.

Dr. Pierre Mornell, author of *Passive Men, Wild Women*, said that 95 percent of the couples he knew personally and professionally described this trait in their marriage: "Whether he is active or passive at work, a dynamo or 'wet noodle,' most men do deal with people and problems all day, so that when the husband comes home at night he's allergic to more people and more problems (especially his wife and her problems)." How can he justify this insensitivity? Mornell stated that "The husband feels that he's worked hard all day and has desperately tried to be a good provider. He thinks: Why isn't that enough? Why can't my wife appreciate me as I am?"[4]

When something happens to cut off a man's contribution—he loses his job or his fortune—the foundations of his relationships are weakened. Two people come to mind whose lives illustrate the potential consequences. In the first case, when Dale lost his "estate" in a business venture that went awry, he couldn't admit to his wife that he had made a bad decision or that he had taken some foolish risks. After all, he thought she believed he was invincible. How could he face her now? How could he go on living with her—a daily reminder that he had failed to give her status and financial security. He couldn't. A divorce followed.

Roy faced similar circumstances. He'd invested his life savings and bet his career on a company that failed during hard economic times. Although the economy was clearly a major cause of his failure, he still couldn't face his wife. He couldn't share his fears and frustrations with her, so he got involved with another woman to whom he "owed" nothing.

The point is that a man's success at work directly relates to his feeling of success in a relationship. This intensifies his stress. One woman in our survey wondered, "Why do they [men] let themselves get so stressed? They work long hours and commit to more than they can do." Researchers at the University of Chicago and the National Institute of Mental Health have identified ten "life strains" that increase men's stress. Three, they say, are related directly to marriage, two to parenthood, and the remaining five to work traumas (being fired, demoted, company failing, etc.). If a man is committed to supporting a family, work failures obviously become more significant to him. So, in fact, men's ten greatest life strains are *all* increased during marriage.[5]

Couple this with the role that the male must play at work: strong, tough, successful, in control, a doer, logical, cool-headed, and unattached. Then he comes home, and his wife and children want him to be tender, caring, loving, and listening. It's a very difficult transition at best.

THE TRANSITION FROM THE WORK WORLD TO HOME LIFE

The world that men feel most comfortable in is their work environment. They can deal with problems according to logic and rationale, and the rewards are tangible and given according to performance. The problems of the work world are clear-cut and the rules are simple—a direct contrast to the world they enter after going home. Perhaps that's why a common complaint in our survey about men was, "They are too rigid—too work oriented. They leave no time for family." By the time the working man gets home, his energies have been sapped, and he has been out of touch with his emotional side. It goes against the grain for him to tune in to the emotional needs of his wife and children.

We are not excusing the male behavior in these circumstances or saying that their responses are correct. We are simply presenting them to help you to understand the male mindset.

Consider these practical illustrations. To be successful at home, it helps to hug and hold. But holding at work can lead to gossip. Making animal noises is great for Daddy at home, but they bring stares if made at work. At work, competing against and defeating a rival may be top priority whereas at home, helping a child win at Candyland is top priority. At home, it makes big points to wrestle on the floor and play peekaboo. At work, the results are not the same. Do you get our point? What is desirable behavior at home is considered inappropriate at work.

Men (and women, for that matter) have to change identities and behaviors as they go from home to work and back. Since working women have to make the same adjustments, you're probably wondering, "What's the big deal?" The big deal is that a man does more than "dress for success"—he *behaves* for success. He becomes his ideal of a successful, powerful man by acting and talking a certain way until he has integrated this behavior into his personality. From then on, he has trouble breaking away from this character.

Living the part has a cost, however. For starters, it produces emotional instability. Indeed, men professionally diagnosed as neurotic have incomes 23 percent higher than "normal" men.[6] Dozens of written and unwritten rules exacerbate this neurosis. Dr. Warren Farrell points out that "no men's room ever features either a couch or a comfortable chair. Coffee, yes; couches, no. And naps—no, no, no. We can drug up and drug down, but not lie down. Not if we're on the way up."[7]

Behaving for success has an impact on life at home and at work. At home he becomes overly critical of his children. He demands maturity and perfection. "When the children of a man on the way up take a break, he tends to see them as lazy rather than well paced, especially if they are sons."[8]

His wife complains that he belittles her problems, making them seem trivial compared to the pressing challenges he faces every day. Her goals become "petty" whereas his become "all-important."

At work, he becomes staid and impersonal. Somehow he can't come down to the level of his subordinates or show that he's human. They sense his aura of superiority and quit talking to him about their husbands or kids, their interests or goals.

Several women in our survey expressed these feelings. One said, "I don't know him very well, probably because he never asks me about me—he's always in a hurry." Another woman, when referring to her relationship with her boss said, "I'm not sure where I stand sometimes in terms of how well I'm doing in my job or even with any personal acceptance. Communication seems unnecessarily impersonal."

Getting ahead in this world requires that a man command the right person's attention at the right time. Impress the boss, and he'll get a promotion. Impress the woman, and he'll get her admiration. And how does a man impress the boss and impress the woman? By appearing bright, resourceful, creative, competent, and strong. By solving problems in record-breaking time. By making his rival look bad. By always having the answer. The more closely he can resemble a hero, the better.

So at work, for example, when one of his coworkers is presenting a proposal for a new project, the man is not always listening. Chances are he's busy rehearsing his ideas so that when the speaker pauses, he can interject some pearl of wisdom that will shift the attention from the speaker to himself.

The role he's constantly called on to play at work rarely includes a talent for *listening*. True, he listens to instructions, directions, and theories, but his objective is rarely to discern feelings (unless that's his business as a counselor or psychologist, etc.). The result is that his analytical, problem-solving mind has little time for showing deference, care, or concern. Listen to this typical scene:

Carol has had a run-in with her boss and sits her husband down to tell him about it. Jeff listens for a few seconds, picks up the gist of the argument, and then starts forming in his mind both a recommended course of action and a listing of the flaws in her approach. He nods his head knowingly and interjects the moment she pauses. He feels like a big guy for having "helped" her figure out what to do next.

She doesn't see it that way, however. She's been thinking through her options all day and still doesn't know what to do. Meanwhile, Jeff claims to have solved everything in ten seconds flat. What's help to him is a put-down to her. And besides, solutions are not what she's looking for. She's looking for a caring touch, an empathetic hug, a look of sincere interest in his eye. She wants to be heard and understood.

Anne Wilson Schaef wrote, "(Men) assume that they can tell us who we are and what we are like. . . . We want men to say,

'Tell me what you are like'; instead we hear them saying, 'Let *me* tell you what you are like.'"[9]

Society tells men that they are to take charge of their lives, to be self-sufficient, autonomous, and in control at all times. A single woman who lives with her parents is considered frugal; a single man who does the same is thought to be a sissy. Rambo is idolized; Woody Allen is laughed at.

Behaviors that reflect powerlessness are clearly no-no's. They include crying or uncontrolled outbursts of emotion, passivity, complaining (which communicates helplessness—don't just complain; do something about it), and so on.

THE MOTIVATION FOR POWER

From a traditional point of view, power is seen as the capacity to make things happen, as are status and control over others. But as a primary motivator in a man's life, power injects conflict into many of his relationships with both females and males. To be caught in a mistake is a way to lose power. That's why men don't like to be told that they're wrong, especially by women.

Power motivates men to become leaders. They tend to see leaders as the powerful and followers as the powerless. For example, all too often, if a man is asked to join an all-female task force, he usually will assume leadership of the group without asking, and the women will usually respect his authority. (Such assumptions are being challenged more often these days, however.)

Thanks to Frank Sinatra, the song "I Did It My Way" has become the theme song for countless men. But that's understandable given that most men favor their ideas and their methods. This becomes especially apparent in a work situation. If the interviews conducted for this book are any indication, most working women have learned that to get a man to agree to do something, she must convince him that it was *his* idea.

We can concur then that the need to feel power is a strong motivator for men. This is one reason why professional sports have become so popular. A man is actually fulfilling a need when he parks himself in front of the TV to watch grown men wage their own private battles for power on the football field or in the boxing ring. He celebrates power by engaging in this ritual hour after hour, day after day. It is his chance to feel power and control.

Thus to be "on top" corporately, financially, sexually, physically, athletically, or politically is *the* goal for many men. And when a man senses that his base of power is eroding, either at home or at work, often his first impulse is to regain the power he's lost by exerting his authority in some other sphere.

Men often grow up relishing power. It is seen as the fruit of the performance struggle—"I earned it." This power is not necessarily derived from an inner maturity or a greater knowledge, but simply from a claim to status: "I am the boss because I am the father." It is often characterized by demanding restrictions and domination. Sometimes it crushes wives and children. It also explains why many men often cannot admit mistakes or failure. They see an admission as a loss of power and control.

Have you ever noticed how many men have trouble admitting when they need help? They'll drive thirty miles out of their way before they'll stop to ask for directions. One woman said she watched two male coworkers waste two hours trying to hook up a satellite dish to their computer. For some unknown reason they couldn't get it to receive the proper signals. Instead of calling customer service, they read the instruction manual from cover to cover. When that proved futile, *she* took the initiative and called the satellite manufacturer herself. Only then would they ask for help.

When asked, "What frustrates you most about men?" one woman replied: "Their unreliability, their tendency to rationalize their inadequacies and/or to blame them on women. If a male employee fails to complete a project on time, he searches for a scapegoat—his secretary, his computers, the copiers. Never himself."

Even more serious, men have been known to ignore ailments or let personal crises get out of hand before getting help. We believe this may be an important factor in why fewer men than women regularly attend church or become a part of a Christian fellowship. Women join churches. Churches foster relationships. Men join clubs. Clubs experience the thrill of winning the championship. It is a statistical fact that when a professional team in a given city loses a championship or play-off game, male violence and abuse of wives and children in that city increases dramatically for the next twelve to twenty-four hours.

THE MOTIVATION OF FAITH

So far we have focused on behaviors or tendencies that go hand in hand with the things that motivate men the most: success, greatness, power, control, and intimacy. Only once have we mentioned love for God as a motivator, which is really not fair to all the men who have put God on the throne of their lives. Indeed, the Christian man who is walking with God will *tend* to be more humble and accommodating and *tend* to show greater respect and love for women. Let us not assume, however, that this is always the case. Just as some men find it hard to accept help, some male Christians have difficulty accepting God's love and forgiveness, which makes it difficult for them to love and accept themselves without first "earning" God's approval in some measurable way. A study utilizing the Rorschach Ink Blot Test showed that men were more prone to fear God and women were more likely to see God as loving.[10]

Sometimes a man carries all of the human motivators with him when he becomes a Christian. So he "performs" for God. Success becomes what he calls "good stewardship" of the talents God has given him. Exerting protective leadership over a submissive wife becomes his way of maintaining dominance in the home. The traps are there for any man, including the Christian, to fall into.

In light of these traps, it is interesting to note that the biblical record shows that God seemed to deal differently with men than with women. His contrasting ways of dealing with them seem to be tied into the different motivational systems of each. Let's pick two Old Testament characters to illustrate our point: Abraham and Ruth.

When God called him, Abraham was living with his wife, Sarah, and his nephew, Lot, in his father's house in Haran. God told him to leave his father's household and his country and go to a land He would show him. Note the incentives God used to insure Abraham's obedience:

I will make you a great nation;
I will bless you
And make your name great;
And you shall be a blessing.
I will bless those who bless you,
And I will curse those who curse you;
And in you all the families of the earth shall be blessed.
        Gen. 12:2–3

Abraham obeyed God. At the age of seventy-five he stepped out in faith toward a destination God had not revealed. He took a risk because he loved God and because something deep inside was compelling him to strive for greatness, to make a difference in the world, and to receive God's blessings in bountiful supply.

Ruth was never given such a specific command, nor did God promise her riches and romance. When her husband died and a famine ended in Israel, God gave her the *opportunity* to leave her home and family and follow her mother-in-law, Naomi, back to Israel to take refuge among her relatives. Her decision to go was prompted by love and selfless devotion to Naomi. Although her name would appear in Christ's genealogy and very few women were mentioned there, God did not find it necessary to tell her that all peoples on earth would be blessed through her. He called her out of Moab so that she could enjoy a closer walk with Him among the Israelites. Given Ruth's gender, is it any surprise that she acted out of concern for another person and the desire to maintain her relationship with Naomi and her relationship with God? And given Abraham's gender, is it any surprise that the promise to be a great nation, to have wealth and power, struck a responsive chord in him?

We have, up to this point, been examining the various aspects of how men strive to achieve. Task orientation can be a positive force. And it is often the quality women admire in men. Most men like to dream of making history. Their natural physical aggressiveness pushes them to want to win, to achieve. Thus, the prospect of finding a cure, negotiating a treaty, inventing a light bulb, solving a crime, or sinking the winning basket at the buzzer is played out in a man's mind in living color. He takes risks and dares to try what's never been done before.

This is not to suggest that women are not equally pioneering and resourceful. But hormonally and culturally the female gender is not driven to succeed in *tasks* in the same way. Certainly the argument could be made that the differences we have explored are made up primarily of cultural bias. Some would argue that they are physiological. We think that they are physiological, cultural, *and* the result of the Fall.

But whether a man's behavior is social or physiological or a combination of both is not the issue. What's important for you to grasp, if you want to better understand the men in your life, is that generally the male motivation factor is both real and different from the female motivation factor.

In this first section of the book we have looked at the reasons men are the way they are and women are the way they are. Some of the differences are a biological heritage that we can't change, but from birth on, the world around us adds to these differences to make the relationships between men and women even more difficult. In the next section of the book, we will help you to determine how much you have conformed to these cultural influences. Then we will suggest a pathway toward a *transformed* relationship between you and the man in your life.

PART TWO

Conformed, Transformed, Renewed!

"Do not be conformed to this world, but be transformed by the renewing of your mind, that you may prove what is that good and acceptable and perfect will of God."

Rom. 12:2

CHAPTER SEVEN

FIVE STEPS TO TRANSFORMATION

> She was taught
> If you don't get married you'll wind up
> a very lonely person staring at the
> four walls.
> He was taught
> If you don't finish law school, you'll
> wind up an object of pity and contempt
> selling ties in an East Orange haberdashery. . . .
>
> *Judith Viorst, "Lessons"*

*A*fter reading Part 1, you're probably thinking that if by some miracle we could accelerate the educational process, letting everyone know what mind tricks social pressure has played on us, then this dilemma could be solved. The facts are, however, that social, or cultural, change comes very slowly.

Our generation, because of quantum leaps in discoveries in natural sciences, increased global communication, and massive restructuring of social and cultural norms, will go down in history as a generation of rapid change. However, for the most part, those changes will be hardly noticeable in the individual male/female relationships you are attempting to cope with.

"So," you may ask, "if the men who make up the relationships in my life are not going to change, why am I reading this book?"

First, the power of God to transform us into new people can transcend thousands of years of cultural norms. God has given us not only a model to live by but also the enabling power of the Holy Spirit to engage that model and see it actualized in our lives and relationships.

Second, we believe that if you can understand the forces

that shape both men and women in our society, as well as our inherent differences, *you can change the way you relate to the men in your life, and they will begin to change also.*

ARE YOU BEING CONFORMED?

In Part 1 we looked at some of the components that make us what we are. In this section we are going to ask you to look within yourself to see if you are operating on what we call a conformed or a transformed level.

Try taking this simple quiz. (Answer yes or no.)

_____ **1)** Do you frequently feel pushed into doing things you wish you had said no to?

_____ **2)** Do you often feel you've lost control of your own life and daily time schedule?

_____ **3)** Do you ever feel a need to prove either your competence, intelligence, or attractiveness?

_____ **4)** Do you, at times, feel resentment toward any of the following roles: wife, mother, homemaker, hostess, employee, do-gooder, peacemaker, cook, facilitator?

_____ **5)** Do you usually work hard at doing what's expected?

_____ **6)** Do you sometimes feel guilty when you leave your children and, at other times, trapped when you're with them?

_____ **7)** At times, do you feel *used* by your husband, kids, or boss?

_____ **8)** Do you feel you have no choice in what you're expected to do in life?

_____ **9)** At the end of the day, do you often feel angry or frustrated because you did what was expected rather than what you wanted?

_____**10)** Do you often fantasize about being in someone else's shoes or being able to escape your present life?

A yes answer to any of these questions indicates a level of *conformed* behavior. Everyone has experienced pressure to conform, and we often give in to that pressure. However, if you answered yes to most of these questions, it could mean that you are being burdened by conformity. In short, you are a victim of dead-end roles.

Go back and take a look at the questions we asked you to answer. Notice that the emphasis is not on the particular activity or behavior (i.e., homemaker, hostess, wife, job, mom) but on the *feeling* you have about that behavior. We asked you if you: "*feel* pushed into doing things . . ."; "*feel* you've lost control . . ."; "*feel* a need to prove . . ."; "*feel* resentment . . . ." The discovery that you are experiencing those types of feelings often means that you are attempting to *conform* to other people's and society's expectations. How a "good" wife is *supposed* to respond, what a "good" mother is *supposed* to do, how a "good" hostess is *supposed* to entertain, how an enlightened feminist is *supposed* to act, how your house is *supposed* to look—all are "roles" or expectations that society or those close to us place on us. When they are performed in response to *others' expectations instead of our own choice,* they are what we've called dead-end roles.

DEAD-END ROLES

Hundreds of the women we talked to felt trapped into fulfilling role expectations imposed on them by outside influences and circumstances. Here are a few of the typical stories we uncovered.

Beth was afraid to be herself in relationships with men. She believed that for love to "survive," it was her job to stay beautiful, thin, and physically fit. And to compete against other women, she learned to do all the things that might impress men, everything from playing racquetball to playing saxophone. She was so busy trying to survive in the dating world that she neglected to develop her inner beauty.

Then there was Shelly. She worked eight or more hours a day, cared for two children, led a weekly women's Bible study, and yet felt guilty because the bathtub was dirty or her husband's dress shirt was wrinkled. Deep inside, she was troubled by her inability to get everything done—and done well.

Irene had a gift for training horses. She loved being around them. In show after show, her horses consistently won the top prizes. Irene belonged in the arena, and everybody knew it— except Irene and her father. From early childhood her dad talked about her becoming a veterinarian. "There's no money in showing horses," he'd told her. "And besides that, I don't want you hanging around those cowboys all the time. They're going nowhere. You've got brains. Why don't you use them?"

Irene became a veterinarian for one reason: to win her father's approval, an indication to Irene that her life had some value. He was a hard man to please, and she couldn't bear the thought of disappointing him—an act tantamount to failure. Five years later, she's still not content with her career choice. She thinks about quitting and going back to training horses, but she never finds the courage.

What do these women have in common? They are being driven by outside expectations; they are victims of dead-end roles. They have a common outlook on life that says: "I have to be outstandingly competent. It is awful when I'm not. I am therefore a worthless individual." They seem unable to separate peripheral issues from what really counts.

Beth felt pushed to always look beautiful. Shelly felt guilty for not being a superhuman mom, wife, homemaker, and career woman. Irene was trying to live her entire life to please Daddy.

These women and countless others have confused the question of "Who am I?" with "What do I do?" Achievements have become the basis for self-acceptance and the rallying point for their priorities. They have confused their "place in the kingdom" with their "job on earth." And now they can't enjoy life because their belief system is telling them that to be loved, accepted, and worthwhile, they must perform the expected role.

One strip in a popular cartoon, *Ziggy*, illustrates this. Ziggy has a problem. We see him collapsed in an easy chair after a hard day's work. He says, "i'm exhausted. . . . i spent the entire day trying to justify my existence."

Consider the treadmill this cartoon suggests: We spend a lot of time and energy doing things we may not want to do, just so someone will say, "Hey, you're something else!" We spend an equal amount of time comparing ourselves to others—and coming up short. What time is left, we spend sleeping. And even then, we're dreaming about new and better ways in which to improve ourselves.

Psychologists call it the Type E-stress cycle, the "everything to everybody" mindset, which compels a woman to labor endlessly for others while ignoring her own compelling needs. It results in exhaustion, perpetual frustration, anger, and burnout—at the office and at home.

BECOME TRANSFORMED

We believe that God has given each of us the power to be transformed. We just have to reach for that power by taking five important steps.

Step One: Reject the World's Influences

Often we accept false beliefs, three of which follow. You can probably think of many others.

A. *"It's always been done that way."*

We can become locked into a role and tradition not because it's the best way of doing something but because "That's the way it's always been done." A classic story tells of one woman who became curious about the instruction she got from her mother-in-law about the correct way to cook a ham. She was instructed to cut off the ends of the ham. When the woman asked the mother-in-law why this was done, she did not know. She then asked the grandmother. She didn't know either. Fortunately, Great-grandmother was still alive, so she asked her. Great-grandmother replied, "That's the only way it would fit into my pan."

B. *"You must look like a model to 'hold onto your man.'"*

Women are given very strong anxiety-producing messages that they must attract a man in order to connect with him and they must keep him attracted to hold on to him. "Don't say good-by to him in the morning in bathrobe and curlers—that's how he will think of you all day." These messages push women into spending a great deal of time and money in preening and may sap important time for personal growth. They also produce self-depreciation: "If I have to fix myself up for him, something must be wrong with the way I am."

In a perfume ad in *Seventeen*, we find a young woman seated on a workout bench—the kind you find in weight rooms. She's dressed in a leotard, tucked up a bit and turned to the side, exposing her long, beautiful legs. Intertwined around her are at least ten shirtless body builders, each holding a barbell with one arm and flexing the other in preparation for a fight. Artistically arranged, the entire scene looks like something out of a ballet. The caption reads "Disturb the peace."

What does this tell a young female reader? That with the perfect body and the right fragrance she will drive men to insanity. They'll fight over her and fight for her.

This delusion is one of Satan's most effective ploys. Keep people worried about their candy-coated outside, and they'll never have time to think about the state of affairs inside.

Honda even had the nerve to run an ad in *Working Woman* entitled "The $6,000 executive makeover." It pictures a woman in a suit leaning against a Civic Hatchback. In diagram form, short lines point to her head, blouse, suit, and car. At the end of each line is a description of the item being highlighted. One says, "$30, neat haircut." The others say: "$50, tailored silk blouse and tie"; "$120, gray herringbone suit, conservative cut"; and "$5799, the Civic Hatchback."

Never mind quality; packaging sells the product. Wear the right clothing, drive the right car, and you'll be a success. Employers will want to hire you. Men will want to meet you. With all that attention, your self-esteem will skyrocket. This outlook on success is dangerously seductive but unrealistic.

The truth is that most women don't dress like the models— and for obvious reasons. On the average, women make only $15,579 per year. Nearly one-third of all female workers are now paid less than $10,000 per year.[1] And the majority of women do not spend their days in the courthouse or up in the executive suite. About 75 percent of the 48 million women in the labor force are clustered in the so-called pink ghetto.[2] Perhaps that's why the majority of business-related ads in *Working Woman* are for copiers, typewriters, overnight mail services, and office supplies.

You may be thinking, "I don't read those kinds of magazines, and I certainly don't use those kinds of tactics." That may be true, yet this kind of thinking permeates every aspect of our culture. Unless you're a hermit, you've most likely been influenced by it to some degree.

Why do women spend such a large amount of time on getting their bodies to look a certain way? How long do you spend putting on your make-up? Or fixing your hair? Granted, attending to personal appearance is not destructive in itself. But at what point do our efforts to look good reflect our being conformed to the cultural ideal? Throughout history each culture has had ideal shapes for women. The ideal image has shifted from the Gibson Girl to Twiggy to Miss America.

Interestingly, a study that surveyed Miss America contestants found that they have become significantly thinner over the past twenty-five years. This is even more remarkable when you consider that the average weight of women under the age of thirty has actually increased over the same time period. Thus very few women have figures as slim as the ideal shape (remember Miss America . . . she's your "ideal"). In fact, it was shown that only "5 percent of women between the ages of twenty and twenty-nine that were drawn from a sample of female life insurance policy holders were as thin as the average Miss America woman."[3] That leaves 95 percent of the American women who are less than "ideal." With all this pressure to conform to the "right" shape is it any wonder that anorexia and bulimia are so prevalent?

C. "Improve yourself. Be better. Go higher."

Self-improvement is the craze of our lifetime. No matter how high you go, the world says "go higher." If you don't believe us, check out the front covers of any women's magazine. We picked two at random, and here's what we got. The first one, *Self*, promises to help you develop the potential of your "body style"; select an anti-aging cream; keep a man from backing off; choose the most flattering haircut; lose weight; and avoid sex-related infections. Our second choice, a recent issue of *Working Woman*, billed itself as "Money, Power, Influence: A Go-Getter's Guide." Other teasers included: "Handle Setbacks without Anxiety"; "10 Ways to Make Your Job Better"; "Aiming for the Top: How to Stay Fit and Look Great at Every Age."

Granted, a life without growth and improvement would be

less than God's desire for us. But you do not have to change, grow, or improve to be loved by God. Rather, you are loved *so that* you can change, grow, and improve.

Few people realize when they are slaves to the false hope of perfection. And the results are always destructive. People who think perfection exists in this world are never happy with themselves, their looks, their accomplishments, or their circumstances. Something is always wrong.

Page Smith, in *Daughters of the Promised Land*, talked about the problem of comparing our place in life to another's:

> Homemaker and wife-of-the-house are rather old-fashioned and opprobrious terms. Much of the discontent of middle-class women seems to be related to the notion that men go off and do something challenging whereas women "just stay home and take care of the children."
>
> The problem with all such discussions of men's versus women's spheres is that the cards are invariably stacked: fascinating job as opposed to prisonlike home. On the other hand we have a large body of literature which describes the terrible boredom and sterility of most masculine jobs. If masculine jobs are so great, one is tempted to ask, who has them?[4]

And yet women can fall prey to the tendency to live vicariously through their husbands and children. When you are dependent on someone, you tend to generate expectations for them. Underlying these expectations is the wish to be taken care of and the feeling of being helpless to take care of oneself. The more dependent I am on someone, the more expectations I will have.

Unfortunately, mothers who are caught in their own dependency teach their daughters to look for a man who will take care of them. The result—the dead-end role cycle continues.

Often these expected roles are taken almost subconsciously. In *The Road Less Traveled*, Dr. Scott Peck described an all-too-typical couples group, in which he was surprised to see that all "defined the purpose and function of their husbands or wives in reference to themselves; all of them failed to perceive that their

mates might have an existence basically separate from their own or any kind of destiny apart from their marriage."

> "Good grief," I exclaimed, "it's no wonder that you are all having difficulties in your marriages, and you'll continue to have difficulties until you come to recognize that each of you has your own separate destiny to fulfill." The group felt not only chastised but profoundly confused by my pronouncement. Somewhat belligerently they asked me to define the purpose and function of my wife. "The purpose and function of Lily," I responded, "is to grow to be the most of which she is capable, not for my benefit but for her own and to the glory of God." The concept remained alien to them for some time, however.[5]

What all of us, both male and female, must come to realize is that being forced to assume a role erodes our sense of self. It will invariably end in frustration, resentment, and/or anger. Do you see what can happen when a woman bases her self-esteem on her job or accomplishments—on pleasing or impressing colleagues and friends? Self-acceptance will never come if it is based on performance. It must be centered in the grace of God.

Step Two: *Exercise the Gift of Choice*

Some of you may be saying, "That sounds good, but there are things that all of us must do that we don't necessarily *like* to do."

That's true. Somebody has to stay home with a sick child. Someone has to empty the garbage or vacuum the floors or pay the bills. Interruptions in our lives and schedules are inevitable. But remember, it's not the *activity* that makes the difference but your attitude toward it.

We all must do things that we don't want to do, *but no one must live an entire life they do not want to live.* When you *feel* you have no choice, that you are unavoidably stuck in your dilemma, then you're in what we call a dead-end role. And your feeling of not having a choice is not based on truth. *You do have a choice.*

One of the most sacred and individual gifts that almighty

God gave to mankind was a free will. God will teach, persuade, warn, admonish, court, reward, and love us—but He will not force us. We are creatures of choice. We choose to love and serve God. We choose whom we will marry. We choose to serve others or be self-centered.

Inherent in choice, however, is the inevitability of consequences. "Whatever a man sows, that he will also reap" (Gal. 6:7). We're afraid to choose because we fear the responsibility of what our choices may bring; but often we choose without considering the consequences. It is important to choose wisely. It is also important to "own" your choices.

Sometimes we would like to hold on to two options that oppose each other. For example, you cannot be a full-time homemaker and a full-time career woman at the same time. To choose one thing means to renounce the other. If you choose one (i.e., to be a full-time homemaker), you should not vacate your responsibility for your choice with the attitude "I had to choose that—I didn't have any option." When you do this, you diminish your personhood as one who can make difficult choices and you live double-minded. Sometimes we try to give others responsibility for our choices. *Yes, our choices may be limited by circumstances, obstacles, even our own values, but we are still responsible for them.*

One mother who was feeling totally overwhelmed by the pressures of a family that was in deep conflict, told Tim, "I long to run away from my husband and kids but I'm trapped. I have no choice but to stay." When Tim confronted her with, "You do have a choice—you can leave if you choose to," she said, "No, I can't. Who would take care of the kids? I have to stay and do it."

"You don't have to. You choose to."

"No, I don't. I *HAVE* to stay."

She and Tim discussed the situation until she was able to see that she chose to stay because she had a commitment to the welfare of her children, which overrode her desire to escape. But by not owning her choice, she was viewing herself as helpless and trapped, and she lost the self-affirmation of making a difficult, but loving, choice—a tribute to her love and sacrifice. When we realize that we have made a choice, we have a sense of mastering our destiny.

Step Three: Have a Sense of Mastery

An important distinction exists between the concept of being in control and having a sense of mastery.

Having a sense of mastery involves vision. Webster defines vision as "a manifestation to the senses of something immaterial." Proverbs 29:18 says, "Where there is no vision the people are unrestrained" (NASB). When we have some insight into God's overall purposes in the world and sense the manifestations of His will, we have a sense of direction.

Having a sense of mastery involves the big picture and allows for a process of change. It does not mean that I have the finished product, only that I am on my way toward the goal. I may not have it all together, but God is working in me and I am learning and growing. Having a sense of mastery involves the development of skills that enable me to deal with my life in productive ways. If my house is in total disarray, I have a sense of mastery when I start with one room and get that in order. It has more to do with my inner world than external circumstances.

Calling

A concept allied to the concept of mastery is *calling*. Romans 8:28 says, "We know that all things work together for good to those who love God, to those who are the called according to His purpose." A sense of calling allows us to see the big picture of God's work in our lives and helps us to find meaning in our lives. Lewis Smedes, professor at Fuller Theological Seminary, related *calling* to "The story that you and God are writing out of your life. It's finding the thread that creates the story line in your life." Smedes went on to say that if we were not true to our calling, we would wind up with a series of "short stories" instead of a "full-length book" of our life. *Calling,* or purpose, in life has everything to do with our identity.[6]

The question is, Why am I doing what I am doing? Am I driven by expectations from outside, over which I have no control? Or am I inner-controlled, choosing to be what I am?

It's really a question of where the *power* is coming from. Am I *pushed* from behind, driven by Satan and the world as it tries to cram me into its mold? Or am I motivated from within, being drawn out by the power of Jesus Christ to blossom and be all that He wants me to be?

In God's reality, success is not an image to be worn on the outside; success is a condition to be felt on the inside. If your heart is pure before God, you are a success. As God told Samuel when the prophet was looking for the king to succeed Saul, physical appearance and social position don't impress Him. "The LORD does not see as man sees; for man looks at the outward appearance, but the LORD looks at the heart" (1 Sam. 16:7). In other words, the Lord looks at motives, desires, attitudes, and convictions. A pure heart fulfills His will.

The Contrast

Let us illustrate what we mean about living life on the conformed versus the transformed levels. Suppose one day you have spent most of the day playing with your preschool kids and everybody has been having a rollicking good, messy time. Mr. Potato Head is in a million pieces all over the floor, the sink still contains lunch dishes, a load of clothes is in the washer, and the rest of the dirty laundry is piled three-feet high in the middle of the hall. One of your kids has just spilled cheese curls on the carpet.

Unexpectedly, the doorbell rings. You open the door, and there stand two members of your women's Bible study—women whose houses you have been in and whose floors you could eat off. How do you feel? If you are functioning at the conformed level you will feel embarrassed and ashamed. You will start making profuse apologies and will run around frantically picking cheese curls off the floor as you talk. Your self-talk (what you tell yourself in your mind) will sound like this: "What will they think? They probably wonder what kind of a slob I am. I'm so mortified. I could crawl in a crack and hide until they leave."

Where did you learn to view things in this way? Your mother? Other women? Your husband? *Good Housekeeping?* Wherever you learned it, it wasn't from the Bible. If you were living at the transformed level, you could affirm that the time spent with your children was top priority. You made a choice to give them your time, which meant the house couldn't be kept as neat as you might like. You're not superwoman. You could feel good about your choice and could redirect your attention from how others viewed you. Easier said than done, of course, because of "conformed" conditioning.

Guilt is a nonproductive emotion. It is a smoke screen to block clear thinking. How can you find out who you are or what you need if you are absorbed in guilt? The tip-off guilt words that we use are *should, ought,* and *have to.* One psychologist called it the "tyranny of the shoulds."

In God's reality, success is our doing what God wants us to do and doing it well. And as one woman put it, "Success is a moving target." The focus of our thoughts and energies changes from week to week and year to year. We must never be imprisoned by yesterday's goals, as God shows us new things about our gifts and talents every day.

Even if you've learned to like yourself, you may still find it hard to *be* yourself. Every time you turn around, someone will be telling you how to think and behave, what to wear, and what to value. And often, what they say will contradict the truth. So to be yourself you've got to know what God expects from you, not what others expect from you.

Luke 10:38–42 gives an eloquent example of this. As Jesus was visiting in Martha and Mary's home, Martha was "distracted with much serving" (v. 40), but Mary sat at Jesus' feet, listening to Him. When Martha complained about Mary's not helping, Jesus told her to leave Mary alone: *"She has chosen the good part, which will not be taken away from her"* (v. 42).

We see two important truths reinforced here: 1) Martha was not the one to decide what was important for Mary (others' expectations of us are not valid). And 2) We cannot be *in* God apart from Him—we must sit at His feet and listen to His voice to determine what *is* the "good part."

Step Four: Renew Your Mind

Do you feel out of control, like a twig in a stream, bumping along? Are you pursuing a career that offers high-paying jobs when your true interests lie somewhere else? Do you ignore the promptings of the Holy Spirit until finally you no longer feel them at all? Maybe you're hoping that these behaviors will eventually bring happiness. But they never will.

Underlying this misconception is misdirected faith. Instead of asking God to give you a vision and the motivation to act on it, you may be building your own vision around possessions, relationships, job titles, or the expectations and values of others. Or maybe your vision is distorted, and you've lost your perspective altogether. Maybe you've given up hope that things can change. But things can begin to change even now, beginning with the renewing of your mind.

Being Renewed

What is this renewing of the mind that enables you to present your life as a sacrifice to God? The word here used for mind can be understood as value system or belief system. The condition of your belief system has a lot to do with the quality of your relationships with people.

Think about this for a minute: Why is it that two people can react to the same emotional stimulus in completely different ways? Let's say that your manager criticizes the way you handled a customer complaint. Because your self-worth is wrapped up in pleasing others, you react by becoming depressed, unmotivated, and down on yourself. And then you blame your negative emotions on your supervisor: "He's impossible to please." "He and I don't see eye to eye."

Now let's assume further that your coworker Elaine gets criticized by your supervisor the very next day for making the same mistake. But she reacts altogether differently. Her belief system says that "iron sharpens iron" (Prov. 27:17), that she can learn from criticism. She thanks the manager for showing her how to resolve a customer's grievance better.

Same events, but different reactions—and different belief systems. Albert Ellis summarized this concept in a type of therapy he called the ABC system. In every human relationship, he said, there is an Activating event, a Belief system through which the event is interpreted, and a Consequent set of emotional responses. To focus only on the event or the reaction is shortsighted. Clearly, some people like Elaine have strong coping abilities and powers of resilience. Others go into a tailspin over trivial matters. Something must come into play after the activating event which accounts for the great differences in reactions. Ellis called this something a "belief system."[7]

When you apply this concept to the way you interact with people, the implications are staggering. Bottom line, it says that you are not a prisoner of the past, that you can alter the fabric of your relationships, not by changing the people in your life but by changing your belief system. And indeed, that is the transformation Paul spoke of in Romans 12:2. "And do not be conformed to this world, but be transformed by the renewing of your mind, that you may prove what is that good and acceptable and perfect will of God." If you can dispute the distorted "pattern of this world," you will be liberated to accept yourself, be yourself, love others unconditionally, find meaning and purpose, and find your place in the kingdom of God.

Step Five: Internalize Your Beliefs

The process whereby beliefs are absorbed is called internalization. Have you ever experienced a time when you knew and believed a certain truth but had difficulty applying it to your life? For example, maybe you really believed the injunction not to be anxious about your physical needs because God would take care of you, but you found yourself worrying about paying the bills. We can believe something on an intellectual basis but not have it sink in at a heart level (or have it penetrate incompletely).

The process does not happen immediately. It happens in steps. The more we internalize God's principles for living, the more content we will be and the less conformed we will be to the expectations of the world. We can learn to be at peace in the middle of a relationship that seems to be dead-ended. Contentment does not mean that we no longer care if the relationship stays sterile, but rather it makes us secure apart from the relationship. We can then function in a completely different way within the relationship.

No matter where we see ourself in the process of learning to live in a transformed way, God's children are given a promise that sustains us at those times when it feels as if we will never get there. In Philippians 1:6 we are told, "Being confident of this very thing, that He who has begun a good work in you will complete it until the day of Jesus Christ." Take heart. Our transformation is energized by the limitless power of God.

CHAPTER EIGHT

YOU ARE GOD'S MASTERPIECE

*I*t was Francine's first counseling session. She was an attractive woman in her midthirties whose hair and complexion were enhanced by the colors of her clothing—probably a graduate of a "Color-Me-Beautiful" course. As usual, Tim started by asking her for sóme background information.

She said she had completed college and had her teaching credentials. She stopped teaching when she and her husband, Jeff, decided to start a family. Francine showed snapshots of two healthy, cute children. Although she and Jeff had the usual squabbles, she was basically very happy with their marriage.

Nothing about her history gave any indication of a problem, so Tim asked, "Why have you come?" She sighed and said, "Let me start at the beginning.

My father was an engineer and my mother a housewife. They both loved me a lot. My father was an exacting man, a perfectionist. He had high expectations for his children. I tried hard to please him, but he seemed to be more tuned into the one C than the two A's and three B's on my report card. My mother put pressure on me in a different way. She was very fussy about how she looked and wouldn't be seen outside our home without her make-up on. She took great pride in the house, but got very frustrated when I made a mess. Whenever I got ready for school or church, she gave me a thorough examination to see if a hair was out of place or a piece of lint was on my sweater. I grew to resent her nit-picking, but rebelling only got me labeled as an "ungrateful daughter."

Once I left home for college, I felt free. But I soon found I wasn't really at peace. When I got an A on my history exam, I wasn't satisfied because the girl next to me received five points higher. I said to myself, "You dummy—if you had just used your head, you wouldn't have missed that one question." I used to spend hours preening for a date, but afterward I wondered if I had talked too much or not enough or if I acted too sophisticated or not enough. I was really surprised when Jeff asked me to marry him. I thought to myself, *Why would a hunk like that want me to be his wife?*

I decided I was going to be the best wife that ever was for Jeff. But it didn't work out as I had hoped. Like last week, when I burned Jeff's dinner and he got upset with me, I felt crushed. I can't bear to take any criticism from him. But when Jeff does compliment me on my dinner or on the way I look, I deflect it or manage to find something to criticize about myself.

When the two kids came along, I was so proud. I take such care to keep them looking good, and I never let them go outside with a dirty outfit on. But when other people tell me how good a mother I am, I think to myself, *If they only knew how crabby I get with my children.* I get so upset when they make the house a mess, especially after some unexpected visitor drops in. I have begun to feel like they are against me.

Let me tell you, Doctor, what happened a few days ago to cause me to set up this appointment. Suzie, my seven-year-old, was playing with her dolls and couldn't see me. I heard her give her doll a good whack and say, "Bad, bad girl. You made a mess and now you have to go to bed. Mommy doesn't love you anymore." It hit me like a slap in the face. Am I really giving her that message? I knew I needed help when it dawned on me that I have the same feeling about myself. *I feel like a bad girl!*

In the last chapter we discussed how we have belief systems that are foundational to the quality of our lives. One such belief system relates to self-concept, an extremely important ingredient of our existence.

Take a moment now to rate your current self-concept. By answering the following statements in an honest way you can have a general idea of how well you like yourself. Next to each statement write yes or no as it reflects your feelings at *this point*. If the statement is true most of the time (although maybe not all of the time), write yes. However, if you feel the statement is false most of the time, answer no.

_____People usually like me.

_____I enjoy my work.

_____Basically, I am optimistic.

_____I do not have many regrets about my life.

_____I am an interesting person.

_____When I look in the mirror, I am generally pleased.

_____I am able to forgive my shortcomings.

_____I am intelligent.

_____I am energetic.

_____I am growing and changing.

_____If I were a member of the opposite sex, I would find me attractive.

_____I am at ease in conversations.

_____I enjoy waking up in the morning.

_____I can laugh at my mistakes.

_____I usually find myself in a good mood.

_____I am kind.

_____I am satisfied with the number of friendships I have.

_____I am satisfied with my appearance.

_____I am not afraid to express myself.

_____There are not many people that I would like to be instead of me.

Count the number of "yes" answers and "no" answers.

Yes _____ No _____

If you had mostly yes answers with a few no answers, you probably have a healthy and positive self-esteem. If you had a majority of yes answers, it is most likely that you really do like yourself. Perhaps you may not be perfect, but you like yourself well enough to withstand most personal problems and allow yourself room to grow.

If the majority of your answers were "no" answers, it could indicate that while you know some of your strengths, you are more tuned in to your weaknesses. If you had mostly "no" answers, it could indicate a high level of unhappiness. You may be experiencing a low tide at this point as we all certainly do. On the other hand, you may be underrating yourself if you feel this way most of the time. It may be that you need to talk with a friend or someone who can share how he or she perceives you. Don't be too hard on yourself or sell yourself short.

In the last chapter we discussed some of the world's messages that might have had a negative effect on your self-concept. Another trap that we fall into is *trying to build our worth on our successes, material possessions, and accomplishments.* This leads us to build our lives around our jobs or our educational degrees. We're afraid that if we were honest, most of us would admit that our paychecks have become a primary source of affirmation in our lives. Our obsession with material goods saps our time and energy.

In a recent demographic survey of *Virtue* magazine readers, we discovered that more of the readers are working out of the home than ever before. But when asked if they were working because of career enjoyment or economic necessity, the overwhelming majority said it was for economic necessity. This suggests that whereas many women have traditionally felt trapped at home, now they are trapped at work. They are caught in a lifestyle with bigger mortgages and car payments. To quit work now might mean foreclosure on the house or repossession of the car and furniture. We have become enslaved to things, and our esteem is dictated by our ability to keep up the image.

Often it seems that the bigger the salary, the less we look to God for emotional support and material provision. That's the trap to which Paul referred in his first letter to Timothy: "Those who desire to be rich fall into temptation and a snare, and into many foolish and harmful lusts which drown men in destruction and perdition. For the love of money is a root of all kinds of evil, for which some have strayed from the faith in their greediness, and pierced themselves through with many sorrows" (1 Tim. 6:9–10).

The world's measure for esteem is fragile. It requires us continually to be preening, pleasing, or producing in order to keep the image inflated. When we are able to function at our best, we can keep things pumped up (at the cost of a great deal of emotional and physical energy), but when we're not doing so well our esteem is deflated.

A NEW DEFINITION OF SELF-WORTH

Fortunately, as children of God, we have a much clearer and unshakable foundation for our worth. Our personal worth is not achieved. It is a gift from God. We have to do nothing to earn it. We either accept or reject it. God must think we're pretty silly at times. He explicitly told us that He chose to regenerate us through the Word so we might stand apart from the pagan world (James 1:18), and yet we don't feel special. We don't act like children of the King.

What is self-esteem? One writer called it the inner strength "necessary to keep trials, tribulations, criticism and critics from destroying our relationship with God." It is "necessary to keep us living around the clock in an intimate, friendly relationship with ourselves."[1]

Self-Worth and Humility

Unfortunately, many Christian teachers and preachers have expounded a particular brand of theology (often called worm theology) that insists that there is no basis for Christians to think well of themselves. And women in particular seem to wind up on the bottom rung of this theological ladder.

In fact, some well-meaning Christians today take issue with the whole concept of self-esteem or "loving one's self." To some, loving one's self is incompatible with scriptural teaching on humility. They tend to equate self-love with a selfish sort of "taking care of number one." Many Christians have been caught in this debate . . . some in a very destructive way.

When we talk about self-esteem and self-love, we are not referring to a worldly narcissism equated with the "me" generation of today. We are not talking about replacing self-hatred with self-centeredness.

What we are talking about is the ability to view ourselves as God views us. Jesus gave us the wonderful parable of the shepherd and his sheep. When one was lost, the shepherd left the ninety-nine and went in search of the one lost sheep. If God's mathematical equation of value equals one, and we are individually created in His image, then who are we not to accept and love ourselves in the same manner that He does?

When Bill and Nancie were expecting their second child, they often wondered, "How can we love another child as much as we do Jon?" The miracle was that Eric, son number two, was a new object of love and joy. Love was not diluted: It grew! Then Chris, son number three, came . . . then Andy, son number four . . . and finally Amy, grafted into the family by adoption. But each child remains unique and is a *specialized* object of love.

So we are to the Creator: original, specialized objects of love.

The Work of the Master Designer

Tim, on a recent visit to the Rijksmuseum in Amsterdam said, "I was awed by the beauty of the paintings of the Dutch masters. When looking at a Rembrandt, I could not help but give praise to the creative genius who painted this masterpiece." Each of us is a masterpiece, a reflection of the Creator's genius. When we recognize this, we can praise the Creator and His handiwork.

What is healthy, biblical self-love?

In *You're Somebody Special,* Bruce Narramore says that biblical self-love is not:

- an attitude of superiority
- self-will
- self-centeredness

But biblical self-love is:

- valuing ourselves as equally important members of God's creation
- seeing ourselves as image-bearers
- seeing ourselves as objects of divine love[2]

The rock-bottom basis for our self-esteem is centered in the fact that we are created in the image of God. We reflect the glory of the Creator. Many Scriptures affirm our uniqueness and worth. Genesis 1:27 tells us that God created us in His image and "indeed it was very good" (v. 31). In Isaiah 51:1 we are instructed to

> Listen to Me, you who follow after righteousness,
> You who seek the LORD:
> Look to the rock from which you were hewn,
> And to the hole of the pit from which you were dug.

How can we be "junk" if we were hewn from God's image?

If you believe, either consciously or subconsciously, that being yourself is not good enough, you are actually insulting God's creative judgment. When you compare yourself with others, you are rejecting the unique design that is you. Your personality, emotional sensitivities, talents, and so much more, are not the product of chance. You are God's workmanship.

OUR SECURITY

Lucy had an image of God that was similar to her image of her father. Her father was an angry, abusive man whom she greatly feared. She described her fear of God, whom she saw (on an emotional level) as walking around up in heaven with lightning bolts in His hand waiting for her to mess up. She felt as if she had to walk on eggshells. Lucy felt unloved by both her parents, and her self-image was dismal. Fortunately, Lucy had a grandmother who was gentle and kind and always had something affirming to say to her. The turning point in Lucy's life came when she was able to stop seeing herself through the reflection of her parents' eyes and was able to see herself through her grandmother's eyes. She found that as the self-love grew, her image of God changed and she grew in intimacy with Him.

God has assured us through His prophets and through His son that a mother would forget the baby at her breast before God would neglect you. Your name is even engraved on God's palm (Isa. 49:14–16). You don't have to win or be worthy of God's love. It is a given to all those who accept it. It is unconditional. The fact that Christ valued us so much that He died for us, the fact that we, His children, are eternally adopted into His family establishes our permanent worth. Psalm 149:4 tells us that "The

LORD takes pleasure in His people; He will beautify the humble with salvation."

Nancie has a cedar chest full of gifts from the children over the years—lumpy clay pots, macramé hangers, pictures of gold-sprayed macaroni. The gifts came home with starry-eyed children, and like all parents, Bill and Nancie oohed and aahed over them and after six weeks or so, moved them to the cedar chest to make room for more. The gifts in themselves weren't that great. It was the children with eyes of love that they treasured.

How often we come to God with our "trinkets," our good works and projects, and hand them to Him as tickets to acceptance—when all He wants is to gather us close to Him and delight over us with joy.

Perhaps you have agreed with what we've said. But you grasp God's messages about your worth only at an intellectual level. You may be asking, "How do I get it internalized so that I know it in my heart as well as in my head?"

GETTING IT FROM YOUR HEAD TO YOUR HEART

1. Stop tearing yourself down. "There is therefore now no condemnation to those who are in Christ Jesus" (Rom. 8:1). Reject the old accusatory, self-put-down thought patterns. You can choose what you believe. Consider the following analogy. For years you have been a slave rowing on a galley. Your master is cruel and verbally abusive. He tells you every day what a worthless slave you are and liberally applies the whip as he "puts down" your rowing. One day your old master is overthrown by a new, loving master. The new master throws the old master in the brig and sets you free. You choose to serve him out of love.

Your new master does not abuse you anymore. Instead, his words of love are like a balm to your soul. While you are rowing one day, your old master comes up to the window of his jail and starts hollering the old abuse. You are so conditioned to listening to that voice that you start to cringe and to do what he says. But then you realize that he no longer has any power over you. You have a choice to listen or not to listen. Our old master, Satan, is our *accuser*. Our new Master, God, is our *redeemer*.

2. Consistently meditate on Scripture that ministers to you in your deepest being. Take some of the Scriptures that affirm your worth to God and write them down. Next time you're in your bathroom, close the door and stand in front of the mirror. Look straight at yourself and speak the Scripture verses to the person in the mirror. Personalize the Scriptures by inserting your name into the verses where it's appropriate. Carry these verses with you on three-by-five-inch cards and quote them often. Here are some suggestions: 1 John 3:20; Philippians 4:8–9; John 15:15; Matthew 6; Psalms 18:2.

One woman who began to grasp the truth of her value in God said, "I can't believe God selected me, but now I'm starting to see creation as an expression of God's love. Although what I'm going through in my life is unpleasant and hard, I'm viewing it as a gift from God. I'm less reactive to other people's negativity. I feel a real safety knowing how much I'm contained in God's grace. I'm learning to love me."

Don't ever forget that in God's eyes we can be human *and* sinful, and He will still shower us with love. If He loves you though you are far from perfect, who are you not to love yourself?

Once we grasp our value, we are ready to begin discovering *who we are.*

CHAPTER NINE

REALIZE WHO YOU ARE

I want to risk—and to love risking. I want to be patient with the redundant, and to embrace the mundane; to see beauty in every moment and detail of life, and to know that life is for living, today, not for saving, not for waiting, not for fears.

Anonymous

$\mathcal{L}$aura, at thirty-nine, was a very attractive woman. Her reddish hair and brown eyes and smooth olive skin were set against the despair on her face. She sat in Tim's office, softly weeping like a child.

"I feel like I've lost *me*," she lamented. "I'm the frame who holds everyone else together. They have their dreams, hopes, and lives; but when I try to do something for me, it gets sandwiched in between their needs. When I sit down to eat a sundae, everybody comes along and wants a bite. By the time they have all had their bite, I don't even feel like eating it. I can't even read the paper without constantly getting interrupted. I feel like I have to be everything to everybody—if I don't it will fall apart. And when I do something for myself, I feel selfish!"

Laura looked at Tim. "I adapt to everyone," she said. "I take on their hurts. If they have a wound, I feel the pain. If they are depressed, I get down. I've found out that I've been so busy adapting that I have lost my sense of who I am. My husband says I'm the Hercules of Guilt. I take responsibility for everyone on my shoulders."

Laura went on to describe another aspect of her dilemma. She feared quitting her job as a realtor because many of her feelings of self-esteem were tied up in her job success. What at home could compare to the strokes she got at work? She felt guilty, however, because she wasn't at home with her children, and she also had a desire to be a full-time mother. She vacillated back and forth between guilt and despair.

"I have a heritage of despair!" Laura sarcastically said. Laura came from a family where there was a great gulf between her mother and father. So she found it hard to determine how much of her hopelessness about her marriage came from the pain and feelings of emptiness that she had brought into the relationship and how much was the result of the problems of her marriage.

WHAT IS IDENTITY?

Laura experienced a sense of confusion in regard to who she was. The name for that inner sense of who we are is *identity*. We are not born with a sense of self—it develops over time. Women's development of opinions, goals, ideas, dreams, and values can be impeded by the cultural insistence that they adapt to what others need them to be. Just as a plant can become pot-bound, with its growth stifled in a too-small pot, we can become culture-bound, locked into roles that stifle the development of our identity.

In *The Screwtape Letters*, C. S. Lewis described how God wants us to be in His image but does not try to take away our will. In the words of a senior demon to a junior demon, Lewis wrote:

> "I know that the Enemy also wants to detach men from themselves, but in a different way. Remember always, that He really likes the little vermin, and sets an absurd value on the distinctness of every one of them. When He talks of their losing their selves, He only means abandoning the clamour of self-will; once they have done that, He really gives them back all of their personality, and boasts (I am afraid, sincerely) that when they are wholly His they will be themselves more than ever. Hence, while He is delighted to see them sacrificing even their innocent wills to His, he hates to see them drifting away from their own nature for any other reason. And we should always encourage them to do so. The deepest likings and impulses of any man are the raw material, the starting point, with which the Enemy has furnished him. To get him away from those is therefore always a point gained; even in things indifferent, it is always

desirable to substitute the standards of the World, or convention, or fashion, for a human's own real likings and dislikings."[1]

What Lewis described as our "own nature" or our "deepest likings and impulses" is our identity. God desires to develop our sense of self, but the world system wants our conformity. Appearance, performance, and status are all goals that are achieved by works. Identity is achieved by the development of the innate personality given to us by God. King David described the way God formed our inward parts and wove us together in our mother's womb, implying that each of us had a unique potential self even before birth (Ps. 139:13).

Taking Inventory

The next step in your being transformed is to take an inventory of your current sense of self. It is important to assess your identity thoroughly. Consider your strengths and weaknesses, your resources, your belief system, your motivation, your level of hope, your goals, and your dreams.

Sit down, take out a piece of paper, and describe yourself to yourself.

1. Who are you?
2. What is it that makes you *you?*
3. How do you feel about your future?
4. Do you look forward to facing a new day?
5. Do you like challenges, or do you shy away from taking risks?

After you've finished, ask yourself what you've discovered. Do you now have a clear self-description which makes you feel good, or do you have a sense of confusion? Perhaps you, like others we've talked to, have only a blank piece of paper. If so, you will no doubt benefit from what we have to say in the remainder of this chapter.

We've found that a woman often becomes angry because "he seems to get to do whatever he wants to do" and she feels *she* has to do what he wants to do also. Rather than trying to get him to stop his activities, she needs to develop her own activities and accomplishments.

If you do not know yourself well enough to have a clear sense of your tasks, options, feelings, insights (the components of any identity), how can you communicate to your partner a clear, concise message? When he asks where you would like to go for supper, "I feel like eating Chinese food tonight, but I am open to your preference," is much more productive than "I don't know. Where do you want to go?"

Taking Control

When we do not have a secure identity, we often live our lives out of control. Being out of control means that we start at tasks from a position of helplessness and feel at a loss to achieve mastery. When we are out of control, our inner hunger is so strong that we have difficulty delaying gratification long enough to get near our goal. This generates a vicious cycle that progresses in a downward spiral. I'm weak—I have a task; I'm overwhelmed—I can't complete my tasks; I feel even weaker—I try again; I fail—and on and on.

Usually there are specific symptoms of being out of control. Eating habits (overeating or crash diets), negative attitudes (being sarcastic, criticizing, nagging, complaining), overwhelming emotions (tearfulness, temper, fears), compulsive spending (credit card buying beyond our means), and our excessive fantasy lives are all examples.

One could also call these *compulsive behaviors* addictions. Behavioral scientists are now finding striking similarities among all types of addictions, be they drugs, alcohol, overeating, sex, or whatever.

Sandra Simpson LeSourd, in *The Compulsive Woman*, tells us the compulsive woman is:

- The woman who volunteers for everything, who can't say no.
- The woman whose TV is on all day long or who lives her life around soap operas.

- The woman whose life revolves around food. She eats too much—or too little. Sweets are often her downfall.
- The woman who is an exercise nut, jogging miles every day, rain or shine.
- The woman who, when she needs a high, shops while debts pile up.
- The woman who is a chain-smoker or a closet alcoholic; hooked on prescription drugs or sex or dependent on male approval for her sense of worth.
- The woman who is easy prey for psychics, spiritualists, cults.
- The perfectionist who never lives up to her own expectations. Her natural drive and energy have become distorted; her motor is running wild. She has an irrational need to do something over and over to the point where she has lost control.[2]

Compulsive behaviors are often misguided attempts to take control of our lives. It's as if we are saying, "Look, I've got everything under control."

Dependent on Others

When we lack identity, we often blame others for our emptiness and frustration. Women frequently blame their husbands for their unhappiness. "It's all his fault that I'm so miserable. I'd be happy if he would just _____ (you fill in the blank)."

Women who devote themselves to trying to meet their husbands' every need typically become frustrated: angry at their mates because it's "never enough" and guilty because *they* aren't enough. In addition, their husbands usually become bored with them. Most of the wives' energy goes into "pleasing" behaviors, which leaves little energy for personal growth and development.

Women have an unfortunate tendency to submerge their identities within their husbands' or children's identities. Scott Peck, in *The Road Less Traveled*, said:

There is nothing wrong with needing each other; we are created with a basic need for relationships. It is when we center our lives around another—when we are so busy trying to get them to notice us—to value us—to meet our needs—that we lose our sense of self. We become dependent in an unhealthy way. People with this disorder, passive dependent people, are so busy seeking to be loved that they have no energy left to love.[3]

Martha was an example of this type of person. She looked to her husband to demonstrate God's love for her. As a result, she kept him at the *center* of her emotional life. Her husband reinforced this by insisting that she devote herself to his needs. "He wanted me to worship him," Martha commented. When she was able to move God into the center of her life, she grew in inward security.

Maybe you are not at this extreme, but you can identify with the tendency. Perhaps a man in your life desires to have you center your life around him. Guard against making him the source of your own identity.

Peck said:

One of the aspects of dependency is that it is unconcerned with spiritual growth. Dependent people are interested in their own nourishment, but no more; they desire filling, they desire to be happy; they don't desire to grow, nor are they willing to tolerate the unhappiness, the loneliness and suffering involved in growth. Neither do dependent people care about the spiritual growth of the other, the object of their dependency; they care only that the other is there to satisfy them.[4]

In our research we discovered that many women experience a deep inner sense of despair, an empty space at the center of their beings. They may experience the depth of this when the youngest child leaves home or when the husband forms a relationship with his secretary, but the loneliness lurks even in the best of times. This emptiness seems to be related to a hunger for meaning, for a sense of self that is rooted and draws up nourishment from the ground of their beings.

This vacuum cannot be filled by centering your identity on any human relationship, an unfortunate tendency of many.

When something disrupts the role of wife or mother, those women who have centered their life on those identities will feel bereft of meaning. They feel more like a function than a person, more hollow than solid. If being "me" means "what I do for them," I will be bankrupt when "they" no longer need me or their need changes.

It is difficult to assess your own needs clearly when you feel you are emotionally starving. It's like going grocery shopping right before supper when you've had no lunch. One woman said, "I'm getting hungrier, and I despise my neediness."

In *Unfinished Business*, Maggie Scarf stated:

> Women are so very powerfully invested in their affec-
> tional relationships—and derive such a sense of self from
> these vital emotional connections—that their very inner
> selves become intertwined with other selves, the selves to
> which they've become so powerfully attached. And women
> feel powerless, humiliated, and helpless to correct the situa-
> tion. It is in women's willingness to put or ante up so much
> of her "self" into relationships that she places herself at so
> much greater risk. For these bonds are so much a part of
> herself, and are experienced so powerfully, that she often
> responds to their loss or disruption or disintegration with a
> full range of depressive symptomatology.[5]

When our goal is to be loved, we will continually be disappointed. We need to change our focus to being the kind of a
person who is loving, rather than to figuring out how we can
hook others into loving us. When we seek at all costs to preserve
our relationships, we lose our sense of self. We become so absorbed in trying to pick up on all the cues from our partner that
we tend to lose touch with our own self.

MARTYRDOM/SELF-CENTEREDNESS: TWO SIDES OF THE SAME COIN

In Chapter 8, as we considered our value as individuals, we discussed the fact that Christian women often find themselves confused over how to act sacrificially in meeting the needs of others, yet assertively in meeting their own needs. They reject the message from the world system that says, "Take care of Number One." But often, instead of developing a healthy self-esteem, they go to the extreme of becoming martyrs, who think in patterns such as, "It doesn't matter if you walk all over me; I'll give you whatever you want." Women who play the martyr role for any length of time generally become bitter and resentful. Although they often deny this resentment, it manifests itself in distorted ways, such as psychosomatic illnesses, alcohol dependence, eating disorders.

In contrast, other women reach the point of exasperation in pouring themselves out for their men. In turning 180 degrees, they become self-centered. They withdraw from relationships by shutting down their feelings of warmth, by getting into emotional or physical affairs, or even by initiating a divorce. Some women vacillate between self-denial and self-centeredness, trying to get their needs met. These options are neither healthy nor biblical, and rarely do any of them work toward the desired result. The following diagram outlines these two destructive extremes:

Self-Centered   ←   *(Extremes)*   →   *Martyred*
(I am oriented to get   (I give up *all* my needs—
what I want in my   others' needs are more
relationships.)   important than mine.)

Let's take a closer look at these two no-win extremes. As we have already stated, self-centeredness is not the same as self-love.

Selfishness is a form of greed. Greed is insatiable, like a bottomless pit. Selfish people are always concerned with self and fear not getting the best for themselves. Selfish people rarely are fond of themselves. This type of narcissism stems basically from a lack of self-love.

A martyr, on the other hand, has the goal of eliciting a certain kind of response from others. One man complained about his wife's martyr-type behavior this way:

> She's always waiting on us at dinner time, jumping up from the table to get something for the kids, who could just as easily get up and get it themselves. Later she'll complain

about it, but she'll never just say, "I'm tired, please get it yourself." She'll harp about how the kids don't obey her, but she rarely takes the necessary disciplinary action to correct the situation. She often complains about feeling sick but puts off making an appointment to visit the doctor. It makes me angry that she gripes about her situation, but always winds up with the "never-mind-I'll-do-it-myself" or the "It's-OK-I'll-tough-it-out" attitude.

This woman is manipulating her situation, trying to gain affirmation and self-esteem by doing everything for everyone. She has somehow believed the false message that performance will win love and respect. While the martyr role may seem to produce the desired results for a time, ultimately the martyr's effectiveness in manipulating those around her will break down. It's a destructive "give-to-get" cycle that will eventually leave her exhausted and resentful.

THE SACRIFICIAL MODEL

An alternative model to the martyrdom versus selfishness dilemma, and one that integrates with Scripture, is the example of a sacrificial Christ. Christ was certainly not self-centered but gave of Himself sacrificially. His acts of self-sacrifice were never done out of feelings of guilt or obligation but were done on the basis of wise choices (based on what He knew were His resources and the other person's legitimate need). Christ used discernment when others expressed to Him their needs. He looked deep into people's hearts to determine what they *really* needed. And He acted according to what He knew to be most loving for the other person.

In addition, Christ acted according to His awareness of His available resources. In more than one instance recorded in the Scriptures He walked away from people with needs. In Luke 5:15–16, we are told that "great multitudes came together to hear, and to be healed by Him of their infirmities. So He Himself often withdrew into the wilderness and prayed." He knew He needed renewal, or He would be operating on an empty tank (a setup for trouble).

As we attempt to follow Christ, we need His insight and discernment: insight into our own needs and discernment with regard to others' needs. As we understand the importance of nurturing ourselves, as we give sacrificially to others, we will be able to strike a balance. Looking to the continuum, we will be somewhere between self-needs and others'-needs.

Meeting My → *(Balance)* ← *Meeting the Needs*
Own Needs ↓ *of Others*

Healthy Self-Nurturance and Other-Sacrifice

Remember Laura who felt sandwiched between everybody else's needs? She decided to start working on learning how to say no. Soon she was confronted with a difficult situation. A teacher from her son's school called her and asked her to switch the day she was going to help in her son's class. The teacher said that no other mother was willing to switch. Laura had, on previous occasions, accommodated her schedule, but on this occasion she had made plans to meet with friends. Her first impulse was to say yes, and she wondered what the teacher would think of her if she said no. She then took a deep breath and said, "I'm sorry. I know how hard you've been working to set this up. I usually don't say no. In fact, I have a hard time doing that. But it is important that I keep my other plans." The teacher was miffed, but backed off, and was able to make other arrangements.

When Laura got off the phone, she felt guilty about saying no, but she also sensed a growing confidence. It was her first step toward a balanced self-nurturance.

One who sacrifices in a healthy way has transcendent goals that are related to the values they hold. They choose to give of themselves out of inner motivations. Our model of this kind of sacrifice is Jesus, "the author and finisher of our faith, who for the joy that was set before Him endured the cross, despising the shame" (Heb. 12:2). We are told to keep our eyes on Him when we are giving ourselves sacrificially in order that we may not "become weary and discouraged in [our] souls" (Heb. 12:3).

If you are in a difficult relationship and are choosing to

"hang in there," remember why you are doing what you are doing. You can continue giving and investing yourself if you look to the potential reward. Perhaps that reward will be a transformed relationship in which you can one day be intimate with your husband. In the short range you can take encouragement in the knowledge that you are modeling Christ.

THE WORK OF LOVE

Following Christ's model moves us toward healthy, Christlike *love*. Love is not a putting down of myself—it expresses my selfhood. I choose to love. I want to love.

Love is work, the expenditure of emotional energy. It is not measurable by how many dollars are made on a given day as is true of the work of an executive secretary or company manager, but it is hard work nonetheless. Women are often doing the work of love in their families, but they have difficulty measuring the achievement. All of the activities that we do with our children—listening patiently to elephant jokes, playing "Go Fish" for the umpteenth time, or chauffeuring the kids to the baseball game—are forms of attention. They require work and can be acts of love depending on our attitude. We can rob ourselves of the self-replenishing nature of love when we do these things out of a sense of obligation (which leads to feelings of resentment). *The acts require the same expenditure of energy, but we experience very different internal results.*

In the *Equal Rights Monitor*, a not-so-funny comic strip showed one woman telling another, "If I spend my days cleaning bathtubs and toilets, my status as a female is equal to a groveling worm . . . . But if I go to work for the sewer company, I'll make headlines as a feminist star. . . . What makes the same job an insult if you do it at home, but an honor if you make it a career?" The answer, "Money."[6]

Paul addressed our tendency to devalue what we see as less honorable. In 1 Corinthians 12, he said that "those members of the body which seem to be weaker are necessary" (v. 22), and are deserving of "greater honor" (v. 23).

When you are doing boring, routine, or menial work, it is helpful to keep Paul's words in Colossians 3:23–24 in mind.

They will help you to enlarge your focus to the meaning behind your labor. "Whatever you do, do it heartily, as to the Lord and not to men, knowing that from the Lord you will receive the reward of the inheritance; for you serve the Lord Christ."

Giving away genuine love renews us rather than depletes us. We are renewed because our sense of personal worth and self-hood is built up when we give unconditionally. Jesus said, "He who finds his life will lose it, and he who loses his life for My sake will find it" (Matt. 10:39).

When we break out of our old patterns of seeking to be loved and learn how to love others, we help the others develop their own identity—to become all that God created them to be. Dietrich Bonhoeffer said,

> Human love constructs its own image of the other person, of what he is and what he should become. It takes the life of the other person into its own hands. Spiritual love recognizes the true image of the other person which he has received from Jesus Christ; the image that Jesus Christ Himself embodied and would stamp on all of me.[7]

True love is a commitment to the development, security, and well-being of the one being loved. If I love you, I will be committed to fulfilling your needs. However, a fine line separates needs from wants. We are not called to fulfill selfish wants. Rather, we must constantly read the needs of those we love, since their needs will continue to change. As John Powell said: "I must be asking: What do you need me to be today, this morning, tonight? Are you discouraged and in need of my strength? Have you experienced some success and are you inviting me to rejoice, to celebrate with you? Or are you lonely and need only my hand softly in yours?"[8]

This is why we say that love is hard work. We must be truly listening, looking, learning, and adapting to needs if we are going to be effective lovers. This will give us the necessary insights to discern between needs and wants. It may be that what is wanted is not what is needed. It may be that the need at that moment is to tell another the truth, which they may not *want* to hear.

The person giving out love must choose what real love is at that moment. Of course we will make mistakes sometimes, but as John Powell emphasized, "More important than the rightness or the wrongness of my judgments will always be the fact that I did what I did because I loved you."[9]

In the end, love is a challenge to the one being loved to mature, to develop, to produce fruit on his own. Love is two people in the give-and-take demands of life, committed to each other's ultimate success and well-being.

CHAPTER TEN

SELF-NURTURANCE

When He had sent the multitude away, He went up on a mountain by Himself to pray.

Matt. 14:23

A fascinating phenomenon among women, who are usually so effective at nurturing others, is their ineffectiveness at self-nurturance. Tim counseled one woman, a loving, caring, and nurturing wife and mother, and asked her to come up with a list of self-nurturing activities. She came back with a blank sheet of paper. She explained that she didn't really understand what it meant to self-nurture: "I just don't know what to do." Tim explained that it was not true: "What is more true is that you do not give yourself permission. It feels too self-centered."

Tim pressed her further to come up with some self-nurturing activity. Finally she said that one of the most relaxing things she used to do (before the children were born) was to take a nice long, hot bath. She sighed and said, "That doesn't work for me anymore. It's not much fun taking a bath with two toddlers in the tub with you." In essence this mother was subscribing to a philosophy that even a hot bath was too much private time for a mother to expect. But is that really true?

A multitude of pressures and demands besiege today's woman. It is no easy task to develop a private life. The biggest obstacle, however, may be attitude. Women often complain about their lack of opportunity, but when presented with the opportunity for private time, many find it difficult to take advantage of it. The dynamics behind this hesitancy are related to guilt and fear. The guilt pertains to the conditioning women have had that says, "You are to make sure everyone else's needs are met, and then you can take care of yourself." Since a "woman's work is never done" (literally), women have difficulty giving themselves permission to take care of their own needs. The fear relates to another aspect of women's conditioning: Women often doubt their ability to be independent, thus fear being separate. One young mother, who had virtually zero time away from her children, was finally helped to set aside some time to go on a solitary trip to a local shopping mall. When asked about her night out, she said she found it boring and a bit frightening. She had centered her identity on her family to such a degree that she had forgotten how to enjoy being alone and she felt lonely and alienated.

WHAT IS SELF-NURTURANCE?

Here's what we mean by *self-nurturance*. We are given two commandments: To love God with all our hearts and to love our neighbors as ourselves. The fulfillment of these commands takes personal energy. We are not unlimited in resources—they must be renewed. We cannot keep giving and giving without running our tanks dry. Have you ever stopped to consider why so many pastors have affairs (often with the women they are counseling)? It's because there is so much demand on the pastors' resources that the pastors get worn out. Pastors are notorious for allowing their resources to wear thin. It's very tempting, then, to start looking for someone to meet their needs, and the trap is subtly sprung. We are in danger when we are emotionally running in the red.

Self-nurturance is the process by which we renew our resources. It's called *self*-nurturance because we are responsible for our own needs. There is a difference between self-nurturance and being self-sufficient. Self-sufficiency says, "I can take care of myself . . . . I don't need anyone else"—an unhealthy independence that is just another version of self-centeredness. Self-nurturance, on the other hand, is making a choice to place myself in an environment or location where I can be nurtured.

Self-Nurturance Vs. Self-Indulgence

Self-nurturance is also not the same as *self-indulgence*. It's easy to mistake self-indulgence for self-nurturance. Self-indulgence feeds that part of us that is greedy and needy. For instance, if a woman has been working hard all day, giving to everyone but herself, she may be tempted to indulge in over-sleeping; eating the wrong foods; or becoming engrossed in soap operas or other extremes that aren't really good for her, thus "rewarding" herself for her many sacrifices. A healthier, more loving way to give to herself often requires self-discipline and denial of instant gratification. She may commit herself to an exercise program; quiet walks; a creative activity; eating the right foods; resisting pressure to get involved when she's already "booked," even though the activity may appeal to her ego. The difference is subtle, and she alone must determine what is self-nurturing. One way to do this is for her to mentally step back, act as an impartial judge, and ask herself kindly (as a friend), What would be good for my friend?

Self-nurturing means that we cannot give others the responsibility to see our needs and respond. Self-nurturance says, "I need to make healthy choices to renew my own resources."

If you have been slaving over a hot stove all day and are wiped out, it is perfectly appropriate to say to your husband, "I've been working all day and I'm tired. I need to take an hour, prop up my feet, and read a book." Hopefully your husband is the kind of man who will respond to your need. But some husbands will not. He may have been too absorbed in his own rough day. Sometimes husbands need some help tuning in to their wives' needs because the needs aren't always clear. At any rate, it is up to you to speak out clearly.

What kinds of needs are involved in self-nurturance? We have our basic needs for food, shelter, and rest. Our bodies are not designed to operate properly without refueling. Often Mom gets run down and starts complaining. The atmosphere of disharmony in the house negates the physical nourishment she is trying to provide. Solomon said, "Better is a dry morsel with quietness, / Than a house full of feasting with strife" (Prov. 17:1).

Be careful to remember that the overall purpose of self-nurturance is to renew our resources to serve God and our fellow man. Any of the things on the list of our needs can become ends in themselves. Men and women can become so absorbed in sewing or watching football on TV, for example, that these activities draw energy and resources away from other things of importance.

WHERE TO BEGIN SELF-NURTURANCE

Ask yourself this question, How would I care for a friend who was in the same spot I find myself in? Or ask the question, How would Christ treat me or respond to me if He was standing here right now? What would He say? If Christ would show love in this way, is it appropriate for us to treat ourselves any differently?

If you are going to develop a private life, with individual activities, you are going to have to do two things. First, you must give yourself permission and encouragement to carry out your activities. This can be complicated by the resistance of your family, so it is helpful to explain your need to them and to ask directly for their support. Second, you must structure the opportunities, or they will never happen naturally. You might come up with a list of possible meaningful activities and form a strategy to implement them. The following exercise will help you get started.

There are five basic areas of our personhood: emotional, mental, social, spiritual, and physical. Take out five pieces of paper and write one area name on the top of each one. Underneath each heading list activities, hobbies, relationships, or recreation that would be stimulating, enjoyable, challenging, creative, growth producing, and fun to you. For example, under *mental* you may want to list a book you have heard about that would be intellectually stimulating. Under *physical* you may want to include a daily walk around the block. Under *social* it might be taking your friend out to lunch (you have been wanting to get together with her for so long, but keep putting it off). Under *spiritual* you may write "Fasting and praying one day a month." Under *emotional* you may decide to write "Take time to write down my feelings." Keep a running list of ideas. Don't let all the obstacles and limitations keep you from writing down an idea. Get it down on the paper before you start to figure out if you can pull it off. Use these lists as a resource for self-nurturing activities. (More on this in Part 3.)

Of particular importance in self-nurturance is the daily nurturance and care of your private spiritual world. If you are going to successfully implement the changes you would like to see in your life and relationships, you must give top priority to developing your relationship with God. The resources available in Him are vital for the energizing of our goals and desires for growth. Unfortunately, this area is often neglected by the harried housewife-career woman, who is expending great amounts of energy keeping meals on the table, children in clean diapers, work assignments on time, ad infinitum. This reminder is not meant to be a guilt trip, but rather an encouragement to take some small step forward. If you are not spending any time at all in a daily devotional, set aside ten minutes a day. Lock yourself in the bathroom if you have to. Just make sure you carve out some time.

Cultivating same-sex friendships is also important. Close friendships can be a reservoir to draw upon in your need for nurturance. They can also be a confidential source of help and feedback.

In order to be successful in developing your private life, you will need to set your limits and sometimes say no. If you allow your limits to be run over, you will feel out of control and resentful. When you are pressured to exceed the limits you've set, buy yourself some time before you respond. Delaying decisions allows us time to pray and to think.

Mary was called by the president of the women's group and asked to head up the benefit spaghetti dinner. She almost said yes but managed to say, "Please give me a few days to think it over." Upon reflection she realized that she was becoming increasingly overcommitted and frustrated. Her main priorities— her relationships with God and her family—were suffering. She declined the job and felt a sense of relief.

THE COST OF GROWTH

Taking mastery of your life and choices may feel unnatural and uncomfortable. Do not expect it to be easy. It is vitally important that you prepare for and accept the fact that pain is a necessary component of growth.

Somewhere along the line, all of us have to make a choice

between safety and growth. When we stretch out beyond our comfort zone and take risks, we are more vulnerable to hurt. If we opt for safety, our growth is stunted. It is a risk to get back on a horse after being thrown off. If you never get on another horse you will never again experience the pain of getting thrown off; but neither will you experience the joy of riding.

Tim had counseled Judy for several months. She had been working to get closer to her husband, and it had paid off. One day they had a special time of closeness and communication. Gratified, she felt that finally things were progressing nicely, and she was anxious to tell Tim about the progress.

The next morning, however, she was surprised to wake up with renewed feelings of depression. She was tempted to give in to the depression, thinking, "What's the use? I had a great day yesterday, only to sink back into depression today."

During her next counseling session, she realized that she had not been allowing herself to feel her own pain. She decided to change her attitude. "I want to get those feelings out," she said to Tim. "They've been inside for too long. I've decided not to be afraid of them anymore. I want my hurt to die in peace!"

When she allowed herself to feel, but not let her feelings dominate her day, she soon found a sense of mastery, and the depression became less intense.

There is always risk in growth, but breaking out of the rut generates new opportunities to learn and to grow. Scott Peck said:

> When we extend ourselves, our self enters new and unfamiliar territory, so to speak. Our self becomes a new and different self. We do things we are not accustomed to do. We change. The experience of change, of unaccustomed activity, of being on unfamiliar ground, of doing things differently is frightening. . . . Courage is not the absence of fear; it is the taking of action in spite of fear, the moving out against the resistance engendered by fear into the unknown and into the future. . . . An identity must be established before it can be transcended. One must find one's self before one can lose it.[1]

The growth process is somewhat like gardening. The first

part involves being planted, buried in the soil. We have to be willing to let go of our control. Jesus tells us that "unless a grain of wheat falls into the ground and dies, it remains alone; but if it dies, it produces much grain" (John 12:24). Deep within our being, in our spiritual genetic makeup, is the potential for growing into the image of Jesus—"Christ in you, the hope of glory" (Col. 1:27). When we are allowing God to work, He will activate that potential.

THE REWARDS

As you put more and more of these principles into practice, you will find yourself handling situations in new ways. And as you grow, you will find that you have a stronger sense of personal mastery. You will be less reactive to others, less hookable—that is, you will not get hooked in by the manipulations of others. In addition, as you develop a healthy personal identity, you will be equipped to transform your relationships. Although these changes will not automatically bring intimacy, they are a prerequisite for intimacy.

One woman who had been very dependent and was afraid of being alone started to choose to spend time in solitude. She described her experience as being like learning how to walk. At first she felt shaky and hesitant, but then her confidence increased. "I'm starting to have small pockets of contentment," she said. "It's exciting because it's a sign that I'm growing!" She was right.

CHAPTER ELEVEN

THE RENEWED MARRIAGE

In Chapter 3 of Part 1 we discussed the impact of the Fall. Adam and Eve were no longer as God had intended. Because of sin, they began separate pursuits: hers toward renewed relationships; his toward the task of fixing what had gone wrong. Sin resulted in the establishment of a hierarchy. And nowhere is this more evident than in many traditional marriages, such as the marriages of these two respondents to our survey:

> "Why does he always have to be right, and make things my fault? Why does he make me feel dumb?"

> "Why does my husband always have to act like the big boss? Why can't he treat me like an intelligent human being?"

Obviously these women are in hierarchical marriages. But remember that this was *not* God's original plan, and when we turn to the New Testament, we find that Jesus' teaching on male/ female relationships attempted to restore dignity to women. In the social structure that Jesus lived in, men were strictly segregated from women. According to the Mishnah, Jewish men were not even supposed to talk to women. Jesus, however, clearly rejected the principle of male domination.

Anne Atkins, in *Split Image*, pointed out that Jesus did not subscribe to the traditional treatment of women. He behaved radically for His day: "At a time when most men were ignoring women altogether except for the purposes of reproduction, Jesus frequently included them in His life and work."[1]

In light of His culture, the scriptural record of Jesus' dealings with women is remarkable. Luke 8:1–3 indicates that Jesus took a number of women with Him as He traveled. Mary Magdalene, Susanna, and even Joanna, who presumably left her husband at home, were among the women who accompanied Jesus. Mary sat at His feet to learn, a place usually afforded only to men. In Jesus' culture women were expected to play hostess, making sure their guests were well fed and entertained. Yet Jesus encouraged Mary to learn.

When Jesus allowed a prostitute into a dinner celebration, Simon the Pharisee was astounded (Luke 7:36–50). On another occasion Jesus allowed an "unclean woman" to touch him, which by Jewish law made a Jew "unclean."[2]

Atkins went on to state, "Perhaps the most telling comment of all is the reaction of the disciples when Jesus, again most unconventionally, had a long conversation with a woman (John 4:6–30). She herself was surprised, particularly since she was a Samaritan as well as a woman (verse 8). And when the disciples came across them both, 'they marveled,' not because he was talking to a Samaritan, but 'that he was talking with a woman.'"[3]

Women were also an integral part of evangelism and the ministry of the early church. Kari Torgese Malcolm stated in *Women at the Crossroads*, "A glance through the Acts [confirms] this impression of the significant part played by women in the spread of the gospel: Dorcas, Lydia, Priscilla, the four prophesying daughters of Philip whose fame was widespread in the second century."[4]

Eight of the twenty-six people mentioned in the greetings in Romans 16 are women, and Paul rebuked the rivalries of women workers in evangelism in Philippians 4. The part played by these same women, who were among the most successful evangelists, is all the more remarkable in view of the fact that in both Jewish and pagan circles it was very much a man's world.[5]

When we summarize Jesus' attitude and relationship toward women as recorded in Scripture, we make the following discoveries:

1. Compared to other literature written during the same time period, the gospels contain a relatively large number of references to women. And remarkably, not a single incident is recounted in which Jesus reproaches, humiliates, stereotypes, or puts down a woman.

2. Jesus called both men and women to follow Him. He

taught women and involved them in His ministry as equal bene-
ficiaries of His blessings.

3. Christ gave women privileged opportunities to play primary roles in the main events of His ministry. The clearest
example is found in Matthew's and John's accounts of the Resur-
rection. Female disciples were the first ones to witness and experience the reality of the risen Christ. They were the first persons
Christ commissioned to spread the word that He had risen.

4. Our Lord repudiated the legal domination of women
that had developed under the Old Covenant. He redefined adul-
tery (Matt. 5:27-30), revoked divorce (Matt. 5:31-32), vindi-
cated monogamy (Matt. 19:3-12), and forgave prostitutes (Luke
7:36-50).

5. The Christian community, the plan for which Christ
gave us, should in no way resemble pagan hierarchical models of
government. This community, which encompasses the church
and the family, is not to be ruled by autocratic leaders who are, in
fact, usurping the power that belongs to Christ alone. Instead, all
disciples, male and female, are to participate in the management
of the church and home. Only team leadership is mandated.
And above all, servanthood is required of everyone.

Repeatedly, through words and actions, Jesus demonstrated
that true kingdom greatness is not to be achieved through rank,
position, or leadership. Only those who are willing to become
like children and servants, assuming positions of inferiority, are
included in the "new community" (Matt. 18:1-5,15-20, 20-28;
Matt. 23:1-12; Matt. 28:16-20; John 13:1-17). Christ is our example. That's the bottom line. And He is the model from which
all Christian men and women should take their cues.

When Christ said, "I have come that they may have life,
and that they may have it more abundantly," He was talking
about the here and now as well as our future with Him in heaven
(John 10:10). Since relationships are the very grid of life into
which we place our experiences, we think it's correct to say that
Christ was concerned about the quality of our relationships here
on earth.

You may be asking, "How does all of this relate to marriage?" Everything we say about marriage in this book is based
on our conclusion that the hierarchical view undermines the de-

velopment of deep friendships and stunts a couple's capacity to cope with conflict in the most creative ways. We feel that couples need to accept the fact that God is working in society to provide us with a gift—transformed relationships between men and women—and that we should adapt our thinking and lifestyles accordingly.

Bill and Nancie relate how the hierarchical view affected their marriage. They had been married five years and, like most couples, had some conflicts. Bill has an ambitious, hard-driving personality and perfectionistic tendencies, and Nancie has a more passive "live-and-let-live" philosophy, though she, too, has strong ideas and opinions. Nancie says, "We were ripe for the hierarchical philosophy. We were youth pastors at the time, and we took our youth group to a seminar that laid out very clearly what roles Bill and I were to fulfill in our marriage. It was easy— A, B, C. I didn't have to think—I didn't even have to work on my relationship with God, as long as I 'submitted' to whatever Bill said. We swallowed every word. It certainly solved our conflicts for the time being. The bad part was that underneath I simmered with anger because I wasn't telling the truth."

Bill continues, "I began to resent having to carry the responsibility for both of our spiritual, emotional, and intellectual welfares. The role—though it worked initially—limits God's infinite creativity in the way He made us, and if we try to live within roles we become stunted spiritually."

MUTUAL SUBMISSION

Knowing what you are working against is just the beginning. You must also know what you are working toward. We think the Word of God gives a perfect model for transformed relationships. In the Genesis account God said, "It is not good that the man should be alone; I will make him a helper comparable to him" (Gen. 2:18). The Hebrew word, often translated helpmate, is *ezer neged*. The word *ezer* means help or helper. The word *neged* means corresponding to or fit for. The overall meaning is a helper who is matched according to his need, one who is complementary. It certainly does not imply an inferior/superior positioning, and our mistranslations of these words have led us to the distorted concept of helpmate. As we already discussed at length in Chapter 2, the typical understanding of helpmate is more a product of our cultural preconceptions than the correct scriptural meaning.

In both Ephesians 5:15–6:9 and Colossians 3:15–4:1, Paul talks about relationships among Christians: husbands and wives; parents and children; and masters and slaves. The ideal, he says, is that all such relationships are characterized by "peace"— meaning harmony—and wholeness. As a prerequisite, however, parties involved must be "filled with the Spirit" (Eph. 5:18), under the rule of the peace of God (Col. 3:15), and indwelt by the "word of Christ" (Col. 3:16). Paul is saying this: If you want to develop happy, mutually satisfying relationships in your life, put yourself under God's control first. Only then (when you are living to please God), will you be able to love, submit, forgive, and be kind, patient, humble, and compassionate—all the qualities it takes to make a relationship work.

A breakthrough for Nancie came when she realized that her number one goal in life was not to have a perfect marriage; instead, it had to be her personal relationship with God, to walk openly and obediently before Him. The satisfying marriage is secondary, hopefully a byproduct of a right relationship with God.

Submission is perhaps one of the most misunderstood concepts in the Scripture. We'd like to suggest that we recover God's original idea by using the term *mutual submission,* which is laid out in Ephesians 5:18–33. Let's look at verses 18–25, verse by verse. Verses 18–21 read:

> . . . but be filled with the Spirit, speaking to one another in psalms and hymns and spiritual songs, singing and making melody in your heart to the Lord, giving thanks always for all things to God the Father in the name of our Lord Jesus Christ, submitting to one another in the fear of God.

This passage addresses all Christians regardless of sex or rank. It says that as the result of being "filled with the Spirit," believers should communicate with each other and with the Lord in the languages of Christian love and that they should submit to one another, literally "in the fear of God." The key question we must ask is, what does it mean to submit to one another?

The word used for *submit* in verse 21 is also used in Romans 13:1, 5 and James 4:7, where Christians are told to make themselves subject to governing authorities and to God. It means obey the orders of a superior in rank or position. But notice that in verse 21, *submit* is followed by "to one another." This modifier changes the meaning. Whereas submission is a vertical relationship between ruler and subject, mutual submission is a horizontal relationship among equals.

The command for mutual submission is not given in a vacuum, however. The verb *submit* is the last of a series of injunctions that follow from the command to "be filled with the Spirit." Together they spell out three prerequisites. Mutual submission is fostered only in an environment where Christians: 1) are filled with the Spirit (v. 18); 2) demonstrate an attitude of continual thankfulness (v. 20); and 3) acknowledge the supremacy of Christ (v. 21). This is where a transformed relationship begins. Verses 22–24 read:

> Wives, submit to your own husbands, as to the Lord. For the husband is head of the wife, as also Christ is the head of the church; and He is the Savior of the body. Therefore, just as the church is subject to Christ, so let the wives be to their own husbands in everything.

In most translations, verse 21 is separated from verse 22 through faulty paragraphing. In the literal rendering of the original Greek text, there is no verb in verse 22, indicating that it derives its meaning from verse 21 and should not stand alone. A literal rendering of the text would be, "Submitting yourselves to one another in the fear of Christ, wives to your own husbands as to the Lord in everything." In other words, verse 22 is merely elaborating on one aspect of mutual submission among *all* believers. It is saying that because mutual submission is the proper attitude of believers toward one another within the church, it should also be the attitude of all husbands and wives who are believers.

"As to the Lord" means that a wife submits to her husband in the same way she submits to the Lord, in loving, voluntary servanthood—not servility. If we use Christ as our model, servanthood is not manipulative, parasitic, self-serving, self-depreciating, conciliatory, or resentful. Put simply, servanthood is death to oneself. For you and me, it means stepping off the throne of one's life and letting Christ rule instead.

In verse 23, Paul introduces the subject of headship. Our first inclination is to assume that *head* means *authority* as it does in modern English. But this assumption is not correct. Conduct a careful word study of the use of *head* throughout the New Testament and you'll find that it never implies rulership or authority (Ephesians 1:22; 4:15; 5:23 and Col. 1:18; 2:19). To the contrary, Christ's headship is clearly defined in terms of saviorhood, servanthood, and nurturance. "It designates the source of life ('Savior'), or servanthood ('gave himself'), and of growth ('nourishes it')."[6]

To help understand this passage, substitute the term *fountainhead* or *source* for the word *head*. It now reads: For the husband is the source or fountainhead of the wife just as Christ is the source or fountainhead of the church.

Now let's build on this concept by examining verse 24. Here the concept of reciprocity—and not authority—is added to the equation. It states, first, that the church submits to Christ. Why? Because Christ is the head of the body. He is the wellspring of the church's life. As a savior and servant (not dictator), He generated it and He sustains it (v. 23). In other words, there's a tradeoff. Christ nurtures the church, and in return, the church serves Jesus. Likewise, the passage goes on to say, the wife gives herself to her husband because he is her source. And as Christ sustains the church, the husband gives up himself for his wife.

If we read on, this concept becomes even clearer. In fact, the requirements laid out for the husband in Ephesians 5:25–33 are tougher than those assigned to the wife. Christ took the form of a servant, humbled Himself, and died on a cross so that men and women might be transformed and made holy. In the same manner, a Christian husband is to become a servant to his wife so that she might become everything God intended her to be, implying, in our estimation, that the husband should take the wife's goals, objectives, and aspirations seriously. It in no way implies that the man should have the final say in all domestic matters. In the words of C. S. Lewis, "This headship . . . is most fully embodied not in the husband we should all wish to be, but in him whose marriage is most like a crucifixion; whose wife receives most and gives least, is most unworthy of him—in her own mere nature—least lovable."[7]

First Corinthians 7:4 tells us that "The wife does not have authority over her own body, but the husband does. And likewise the husband does not have authority over his own body, but the wife does." Mutual submission means that we are to regard the other as having a form of ownership over us. We submit ourselves to each other in order to meet each other's needs—to please each other.

THE APPLICATION

What is the implication of these teachings for our relationships? Marriage is a God-designed institution that facilitates the shaping of each partner into the image that God intends. In order for this process to be effective, each of the partners must be willing to be transformed, and each must be willing to be used to transform. Proverbs 27:17 tells us that "As iron sharpens iron,/ So a man sharpens" another. Do you view yourself as someone who is forged and ready for that kind of interaction, or do you feel as soft as butter? Do you fear the pain of the sharpening process?

Nancie says, "It was somewhat scary for us to move from a hierarchical marriage to one of mutual submission. We had to learn to release each other. And we had to let go of some of our unrealistic expectations. We still have a ways to go, but we love and respect each other more; we have a more interesting marriage; and we feel like we're pulling together as a team."

This is a critical point. "One flesh" does not mean identical outlooks on life. Dr. John Cuber, sociology professor at Ohio State University, said in regard to the marriage of equals:

> While the husband and wife find the greatest pleasure in each other's company it is not because they have identical outlooks and treasure complete unanimity. On the contrary,

each delights in the other's individuality, prizing the unique qualities that permit each to see the world a little differently.[8]

Unfortunately many couples get locked into relationship traps, which are contradictory to God's plan for marriage. They don't start out that way when they first get married, but they often drift into frustrating patterns.

THE PATTERNS WE DRIFT INTO

It is fascinating to ask an estranged couple what it was that attracted them to their mates at the beginning of their relationship. Invariably the qualities that attracted them are the same qualities they complain about. Her "bubbliness and spontaneity" have turned into "overemotionality and impulsivity," and his "steadiness and objectivity" have become "stodginess and cold logic."

It is no accident that the "overemotional" woman marries the "unemotional" man. Both are intuitively seeking that which is missing in themselves. They seek to be complementary, but instead they sometimes intensify their differences. Do you remember the seesaw rides you used to take as a child? What happened when you sat opposite another child who moved farther from the center? You had to move farther from the center yourself to keep the seesaw in balance. The seesaw phenomenon happens just the same with couples. As he moves away from his feelings, she becomes more emotionally expressive. As she becomes more emotional, he reacts by shutting down his emotions even more.

Since most men have learned how to tune out their mothers effectively, don't expect that complaining and nagging will elicit a positive response. At best, you are likely to get a wall of silence. At worst, you may get an angry push-off. Women in the *Virtue* survey expressed frustration with this. One woman, typical of many, said, "He tunes me out . . . he doesn't listen." Another wrote, "He just watches his precious TV and gets angry when I tell him I need help with the kids."

When you try to change a person who does not want to change, you generate more resistance than was originally there.

A female's nagging, complaining, or becoming hysterical will usually trigger the male's response of clamming up, withdrawing, or blowing up. You will end up feeling even more helpless and stuck. If you find yourself in this vicious cycle, calm down, take a mental step backward, and look more objectively at the patterns between you and your partner. If you can begin to see the cycle, the moves and corresponding countermoves, you have a start on breaking out.

Couples create a stand-off when each partner acts like "my way is the right way—I expect you to change, and I am not going to be the one to change." When this happens the relationship goes nowhere.

One of the ways we manipulate and control each other is to "push buttons," as Mary and Ralph did when they started arguing about Mary's "favorite" issue—money. Ralph accused Mary of overspending the budget, and Mary accused Ralph of being tight with money for the household. They hooked into each other's tender spots. Ralph pushed Mary's "self-esteem button" and said, "I bust my buns eight hours a day to make ends meet, and you've got the time to shop wisely. Why don't you spend more time shopping for bargains, instead of jumping around in leotards with a bunch of women at aerobics?" Mary retorted with a shot aimed at Ralph's "guilt button." "That's easy for you to say. I wasn't the one who bought a $300 power saw!"

One of the most common ways of spouse control is through money. Who gets the checkbook? Who gets to *balance* the checkbook? Who decides to spend, and how do we react to each other when we spend? One woman said, "I am fearful of spending money. When I do, I can visualize the disapproving look on his face." Another woman's husband took the checkbook away when he was feeling an erosion of his control in the relationship.

Many women feel as if their marriage is a slowly sinking ship. They constantly have to work the bilge pump to get the water out of the hold. Emotionally and physically exhausted, they insist they can't stop pumping because if they ever do, the ship will sink.

When we are doing something for another person because "he or she wants me to do it" rather than "I choose to do it," we generate the belief in our minds (however unconscious) that they are in our debt, and we generate expectations for them. We may "sacrifice" (of the martyr variety) for the other, but we are getting some sort of payoff. The payoff may be a feeling of superiority, or it may be the satisfaction of knowing that another is in our debt.

It is important not to try to force a certain response to our acts of giving. Rather we should allow the other to choose a response. Men often feel smothered by their wife's "love." If your partner is experiencing these feelings, you may want to examine whether you are showing dependence or love. It is easy to fool ourselves into thinking we are loving when we are actually giving in order to get back. The Lord warned the prophet Jeremiah that "The heart is deceitful above all things, / And desperately wicked; / Who can know it?" (Jer. 17:9) Fortunately, He also stated that "I, the LORD, search the heart, / I test the mind" (Jer. 17:10).

If you are receiving "I'm-feeling-smothered" messages from others, ask God to reveal to you where your love might have strings attached. Remember, true love sets the other free—it "does not seek its own" (1 Cor. 13:5). It facilitates the development of the other person's identity—it is not jealous (1 Cor. 13:4). It forgives the failings of the others (lack of appreciation, for example). It does not take into account a wrong suffered (1 Cor. 13:5).

When you sacrifice for your husband with the expectation that he will reciprocate, you put an implicit pressure on him. He is likely to resent this subtle demand and unlikely to respond in the way that you hope.

BREAKING OUT

As difficult as it may be, you need to break out of the cycle. Stop doing the typical behavior. Once you stop, you will discover how much energy you have been pouring into behaviors that do not get you where you want to go. When you halt your part of the dance, you will find that you have emotional energy available to reinvest in new behaviors.

When women get into the marriage dilemma that we have just described, they often see only two alternatives. One is to try to take control; the other is to passively be a victim. Neither attains intimacy with a man. The passive option is characterized by peace-at-any-price behavior. This kind of behavior does not rock the boat, but neither will it get others to take you seriously.

Although you may feel stuck in a relationship that is beyond hope, although you may feel powerless to bring change, although you may feel the desperation of having tried everything, you need to hear something loud and clear. *You can improve your relationship with almost any man by the choices that you make.* The same principles we discussed in Chapter 8 about taking ownership of your choices apply to your relationships in this context. When you change *you*, the relationship is automatically changed. It is no longer the same. This is not to say that you are completely responsible for your relationship, but rather that you are responsible for you, your insights, talents, gifts, energies, and emotions. We are not absolved of the responsibility to invest our resources because another person withholds.

To some, this may sound like an invitation to be used and abused. You may be thinking, "I'm tired of being a victim." But this is *not* an injunction to be victimized. Rather it is an injunction for you to take positive steps toward improving your relationships by changing you.

We have just outlined some principles that can transform our relationships if they can be put into action. "Easier said than done," you may be saying. That's a good point. Why is Christian marriage often not like the biblical model we have described? Because we Christians have opted for the easier worldly pattern rather than the more difficult biblical standard. As one woman said, "Whoever said that good marriages do not require a lot of work was either not married very long or not married at all."

At this point you may agree with the challenge but wonder how to pull it off in your own life. Each of us needs to overcome obstacles. In the next chapter we hope to help you translate these principles into practical action.

CHAPTER TWELVE

LETTING GO

But let there be spaces in your togetherness,
And let the winds of the heavens dance between you. . . .

*Kahlil Gibran, The Prophet**

*N*orma and Al were locked into a no-win power struggle in their marriage centered around household jobs that Norma wanted Al to do. Norma didn't have the know-how to fix the cabinet door, and Al kept making promises to fix it and do the many other undone chores. You see, Al was a procrastinator. The more Norma nagged, the more Al seemed to drag his feet. In fact, Norma's nagging actually gave him ammunition to keep him from doing the jobs. The issue became "Norma the Nag" instead of the real issue, fixing the cabinet. The more she pushed, the more stubborn he became. He kept the focus on her rather than why he wasn't following through on his commitment. Finally Norma realized the "no-win" nature of the interaction. She went to Al and said, "Al, you know how much I'm bugged by the cabinet door that is falling off. It is a real source of irritation to me. I will be calling Tom, the handyman, on Monday to ask him to fix it next week. I really don't want to spend the money on this, but I'd rather spend it than stay irritated." To her surprise, Al got out the tools and fixed not only the cabinet door but also the leaky faucet. Norma said, "I stopped relying on him and he became more reliable."

Have you ever found yourself in a no-win situation with your husband and wondered how you got there and how to get out? In many aspects of our relationships, we need to learn to let go.

---

*Kahil Gibran, *The Prophet* (New York: Alfred A. Knopf, 1923).

Remember in Part 1 we discussed how women are trained to be feelings oriented and men are trained to be performance oriented. Our skills are often more highly developed in one direction or the other. As a result, we try to compensate for each other. Women often end up doing the emotional work for men, and men often end up doing the rational, problem-solving work for women. This results in our preventing each other from the development of our wholeness. If you hope that your mate will develop his feelings, stop overcompensating for his weaknesses. Once you stop doing all of his emotional work, he will gradually develop the skills and confidence to do some of his own.

TRANSFER RESPONSIBILITY

The wife also tends to assume responsibility for keeping the relationship going with the husband's family. Wives send the cards, pick out the birthday gifts, and make the calls to his parents. "Did you remember to call your mother?" One woman found herself cooking her mother-in-law's meals, cleaning her house, and fixing the older woman's hair. When something needed to be done, whom do you think the mother-in-law called?

When the daughter-in-law had finally had enough, she told her husband he would have to take care of his own mother. She felt a great deal of guilt. What if the mother-in-law suffered rejection when she stopped doing all she was doing? *Am I being selfish?* she mused.

Her husband did not understand. After all she had been doing this for years, and this kind of thing was "woman's work" wasn't it? "I go out and bring home the bacon, and you stay home and have time for this sort of thing." When his wife stood her ground, however, he started to take more of an interest in his own mother's needs.

Women typically get hooked into assuming too much responsibility in the raising of kids. When Junior comes in with a problem, Mom is usually the one who is expected to have the listening ear and the comforting words. Or if the child goes to the father and he becomes exasperated and impatient, the mother jumps in to give the emotional support. Most men then withdraw from the involvement.

We are not doing our spouses any favors when we protect them from certain tasks and thus prevent them from developing positive character traits that lead to wholeness.

Drawing the Line

It is terribly difficult to know where to draw the line. An excellent rule of thumb to apply in these situations is to ask yourself one question before responding to an expressed need: What is the most loving thing I can do for this person?

For example, one couple sought help for their marriage when the husband was demanding to have sex practically every evening and she was feeling totally worn out and used. He would hit her over the head with the verse about "not depriving your mate" (a handy club when taken out of context), and she boiled. She attempted to meet his emotional needs, but they seemed insatiable. As it turned out, he had a great deal of insecurity stemming from childhood wounds. What he said he needed— sex—and what he really needed—an in-depth healing—were two different things. No amount of sex could have fulfilled his need.

In order to apply this principle, you must trust your own ability to discern (your natural intuition), which may take some time and practice. Allow for mistakes, negative responses from others, and the space to tune in to the "still, small voice of God." Most needs do not have to be met immediately (although the demanding voices in our lives tell us otherwise). Time allows men the opportunity for their own introspection—a necessary element of growth. Men, due to their fear of their own dependency strivings, get desperate at times. To avoid looking at the emotional hunger, an unconscious male strategy is to project blame onto the woman who is depicted as being "cold, unresponsive, and deprivational." When you capitulate to the pressure to meet your man's need against your better judgment, you reinforce a destructive pattern and breed resentment in your own heart. It is not helpful to confront the man with accusations about the childish nature of his demands. It is much better to stand your ground with a message that centers on your choice not to meet that need and an explanation about what is going on in you.

Do not try to be your husband's mother. You are not his mother, and you do not have to assume responsibility to act like one. Besides, when you do (even when he asks for mothering) he will resent you.

If you expect him to be strong and capable of handling every problem, it may be difficult for you to allow him to feel helpless and confused, but you can't expect men to be strong and silent one minute and open and emotional the next. This double message causes confusion and frustration for men.

Releasing Control

Letting go is unnatural for many women. After being trained all one's life to be the caretaker, it goes against the grain to release the controls when the relationship feels like it is on a collision course. Talk about feeling out of control! The feeling is similar to the response we make when our car skids on a patch of ice. Our tendency is to whip the wheel in the opposite direction, but the helpful response is to steer into the skid.

Eileen was frustrated every year when her birthday rolled around. Each year she and her husband ended up in a fight because he would just run out at the last minute and get something. She felt unloved. This year she decided to do it differently. She planned a special evening at a restaurant she loved to go to. She made the reservations and told her husband when they would be going. To her surprise he participated willingly, and they had a great time.

Women need to make an emotional "Declaration of Independence" to themselves—a positive self-statement. One self-statement that you might repeat over and over to yourself until it sinks in is, "I am responsible for myself; he is responsible for himself." If you do not believe the first part and instead believe that anyone else is responsible for making you happy, you will end up sowing the emotion of anger: "He let me down again; you just can't trust men."

If you do not believe the second part and feel like you are making his life miserable and always letting him down, you will end up sowing the emotion of guilt: "I can't ever please him; there is something wrong with me." These behaviors result in a no-win situation.

When you have chosen to change, the ball is in your partner's court, so to speak. Do not try to choose for him. One woman expressed doubt about whether her husband would even try. He didn't like the way the relationship was going—"He's perfectly unhappy with the way things have been"—but he seemed unwilling to do anything about it.

This is where faith comes in. We can work toward change, but it is essential to have faith that God is working in our relationships. We are His change agents, but the Spirit empowers the change. We take responsibility for what is under our control, and we let God handle that which is His. You are not strong enough to change another person's heart. Allow God to do His work.

Betsy told Tim during a counseling session, "I stopped telling God how to do things. I realized I was in no position to advise." This was the beginning of Betsy's learning how to let go.

Her husband, George, loved his hobbies and recreation. When he pursued them, he did so totally. Fly-fishing was his latest addiction. He spent every evening tying flies and every weekend fishing. The burden of caring for the kids fell completely on Betsy. Normally, she would nag at George about his compulsion, but this time she did not say anything. Instead, she started praying about it daily. She was dumfounded when one day George came to her and said, "I realized I've been out of control with my hobby. I've decided from now on I'll just do my fly-tying after the kids are in bed."

Dietrich Bonhoeffer said, "I must release the other person from every attempt of mine to regulate, coerce, and dominate him with my love. The other person needs to return his independence of me; to be loved for what he is, as one for whom Christ became man, died and rose again, for whom Christ brought forgiveness of sin and eternal life."[1]

If you have been in a push-pull relationship, it is very helpful to give your partner a clear "letting go" statement. For example, Betsy stated it like this: "George, I realize that I have been trying to change you, to make you into the kind of husband that

I wanted. That has put pressure on you and I have not accepted the way you choose to be. I ask your forgiveness for pressuring and nagging you. I will do my best to change this. I do have needs that are unfulfilled. Some of them are needs that you are capable of meeting, and some are needs that others can meet. Some only God can meet. I have been looking to you to make me happy and that is not right. I will continue to express certain needs to you, but I will not try to make you meet those needs. You will have to choose how you wish to respond." Betsy began to notice a change in George's attitude almost immediately.

THE REBUILDING PROCESS

When you start to change your ways of interacting and behaving, the equilibrium of your relationship will be disturbed, which can be difficult and threatening for you. Expect comments from your husband like, "I think you're getting worse." Sometimes a spouse may be determined to keep the relationship the same. In these instances you can expect defensiveness and attempts to discount what you say. It is important to keep your bearings on your vision for the marriage, which is what Tim suggested to Martha.

Martha started to work on her attitudes and was making positive strides to let go of her need to control her husband, Norm. He started to respond positively to her efforts. Then came a regression. He stepped back into old patterns. Martha lost perspective on what she was working toward and became very depressed. Only after refocusing on the big picture (remembering what she was working toward and why and being able to affirm her overall gains) was Martha able to regain a sense of mastery in her life.

As you grow and your mate doesn't, you can expect the gap between you to widen temporarily. This can be very upsetting. After all, your intent is to get closer, not further apart. However, you may be breaking out of a relationship rut ahead of your partner.

When Nancy started changing, Frank started getting more sullen and resentful. She didn't understand why until he blew up and told her he felt bored in his daily routine and trapped in his job. She was learning new things and was meeting interesting new people. She had to laugh to herself. Those were the same feelings she had about him before she got out of her rut. She had been jealous of *his* life.

Sometimes a husband will sit back for a while to see whether the changes in you are real. When a relationship gets stuck, a kind of inertia sets in. It takes a number of accumulated changes to break it free.

Building Trust

When you find yourself on an emotional roller coaster with your partner, you can stop the ride by moving from mutual fault-finding to mutual problem solving. You might begin by saying, "We are getting nowhere by blaming each other. Can we sit down and come up with some possible solutions?" In other words, drop blaming, and replace it with self-questioning: What is my part of the problem? How can I change me?

Perhaps the trust between you has been greatly eroded, and an atmosphere of fear has entered your relationship. Ask yourself, What can I do to rebuild his trust in me? It is highly unlikely he will share his deepest emotions with you if he doesn't trust you.

In some situations where real wounds have been created, sincere apology is a form of trust-building. We know how hard this is to do, especially when the other person has been hurtful and has not acknowledged it. Maybe he has hurt you ten times for each one hurt you have caused. You cannot keep score or you will find it difficult to apologize for your hurtful act.

When your mate makes even the smallest movement toward the goal of intimacy and openness, reinforce it with a word or deed. James started to open up as he and Jean drove back from the coast. She was ecstatic but tried not to act too enthusiastic. Suddenly they found themselves embroiled in a fight. Jean was confused as to how things deteriorated so quickly. What happened was that James started getting scared with his self-disclosure and subconsciously felt the need to start a fight. Later, as they talked, he reflected on his puzzlement about why communication seemed to be so difficult. He became more complimentary of her, and she purposely tried to build him up. She told him how much she liked being with him and praised him. They had turned the corner in their relationship.

This will be very difficult if you are harboring bitterness because you will find it hard to see the small and tender shoots of growth. In Hebrews 12:15 we are warned to take care that no "root of bitterness" springs up to cause trouble.

When we are frustrated we often lose sight of the good things about our relationships. It helps to thank God for the simple, daily enjoyments of partnership.

Some of you, as you read this, may be saying to yourself, "That's all well and good for a lot of people, but you don't know my husband." Some relationships have so much conflict that they seem hopeless. Some women have been expending so much energy trying to keep the marriage afloat that they are exhausted. We are not advocating that you "just pump harder," but we are suggesting that you give this new way of relating a chance.

Relationships can be transformed by the grace of God. It takes time, emotional pain, hard work, and endurance. There are no quick fixes. But two people who are committed to each other and to God can make a change.

PART THREE

Living the Transformed Life

Instead of minimizing our differences
    let us maximize them
Instead of denying that you are better at this
    and I am better at that,
Let us take full advantage of our special skills
    and recognize the weaknesses
    in order either to work on them
    or turn to what we do best
It is OK with me
    that most men have better spatial skills
    and that most women are better at verbal skills
I can accept that most men are concerned with
    objects
    and most women with people
That boys excel at gross motor coordination
    and girls at manual dexterity
That males are good at problem-solving
    and females process information faster
I like our differences!
As you shovel the driveway
    I fix you hot soup
As you drive at night
    I keep you awake
As you carry the suitcases
    I check in at the counter

You figure our taxes
    I decide on our budget
You vacuum
    I dust
You turn the mattress over
    I water the plants
You chop the onions
    I add the spices
You go marketing . . .
    but with my shopping list
I buy you ties
You know how to cure the ills of the world
    I know how to cure your ills
You know what children ought to do
    I know how they are
You know about driving in snow
    I know you should wear a scarf
You show me how much you love me
    I tell it to you
I could not do well what you do so well
    nor could you do what I do
I like me as me
    and you as you.

Natasha Josefowitz, "Patterns," in Is This Where I
Was Going?

CHAPTER THIRTEEN

STRATEGY FOR SUCCESS

"Forgetting those things which are behind and reaching forward to those things which are ahead, I press toward the goal. . . ."

Phil. 3:13, 14

*I*n the last section we sought to give you a blueprint for conceptualizing the changes that would be necessary in order to transform first, yourself, and, second, your relationships. In this section we want to help you apply that model to your life, with some very practical steps—specific ways to begin.

We begin in this chapter with three basic steps as a starting point:
1. Letting go of the past
2. Setting goals
3. Taking life in phases

1. LETTING GO OF THE PAST

Tim, in his counseling, has found that hope best indicates whether or not a person will successfully change. The thing that most effectively stifles hope is a sense that no matter how hard I try it will not make any difference. When we have hope, in contrast, we have a sense that "all things [can] become new" (2 Cor. 5:17). Not only can I change but others can too.

One of the essential steps in cultivating hope is letting go of the past. Letting go of the past is not the same as pushing our feelings about the past out of our awareness. In fact, it is essential that we not do that. If we do not understand our past, we usually end up repeating it. We get caught in endless vicious cycles that

138

sap our energy and breed despair. Hopefully, at this point, you have a much greater understanding of how things have happened the way they have and are ready to forgive and forget the hurts that have been done to you as well as the hurts you have caused.

This is a story from Bill's pastoral experience. Rachel was bitter. For over six years she had been a faithful wife to her husband, Dave. For three of those years she had worked while Dave went to law school. The next year she gave birth to their first child and just six months ago gave birth to their second.

She began to realize that their marriage had difficulties three years ago. Dave became both irritable and aloof. She compensated by trying to do more things to please him, acting the part of the perfect wife, hostess, and mother. But the more she tried, the more irritable and withdrawn Dave became.

Right after their second baby was born, Dave agreed to see a counselor. He and Rachel both wanted to try to save their marriage and family.

During the counseling, Dave confessed to having a brief affair with one of the women he had met in law school about three years before, during Rachel's first pregnancy. He said that his ongoing guilt for what he had done made him feel unworthy of a woman like Rachel. That's why he had become more irritable and withdrawn. Dave's guilt seemed to be sincere and heartfelt. He begged Rachel for her forgiveness. He seemed tremendously relieved and wanted to move on in their marriage.

At first Rachel was stunned and deeply hurt at the news of Dave's affair. After a few weeks her hurt turned to anger and bitterness. "How could he possibly have done this while I was carrying his child! I put him through school, I carried his babies, I tried to be the perfect wife and mother, and he did this to me!" After weeks of counseling, Rachel confessed that she was not sure she could ever forgive Dave.

Many offenses are not as big as Dave's. Often little things add to our hurt and anger. Verbal put-downs, disregard for our opinions and ideas, selfishness, lack of communication, and other daily offenses can stack up (especially if you keep score) until finally there seems to be too much to forgive.

The truth is, whether it's a big mistake like Dave's or little things that have stacked up, unless you can forgive and let go of the past, your marriage has little chance of survival and even less chance of being happy and well adjusted.

We are not asking you to *forget* the past. That is probably not possible. But it is possible to *let go* of the past. Letting go means forgiving.

The basic foundation of our faith is forgiveness. Without God's promise of complete forgiveness, we simply have no basis for our Christian faith. God not only set the example and pattern of forgiveness, but He frequently told us to follow that pattern. In Jesus' own example of effective prayer, He stated, "Forgive us our debts, as we forgive our debtors" (Matt. 6:12). God left no doubt about His expectations of forgiveness.

The apostle Paul, in Ephesians 4:32, said, "Be kind one to another, tenderhearted, forgiving one another, just as God in Christ also forgave you."

Forgiveness is expected by God not only in the marriage relationship but also in *all* relationships. According to Scripture, harboring anger, resentment, bitterness, or any offense committed against us is a sin. In marriage especially, the unresolved offenses and negative patterns that have built up over the years—all the hurtful words, all the acts of infidelity, and all the lies and inconsistencies—simply must be forgiven if your life is ever to be blessed by God. If you do not forgive, you can never totally let go and be released. Unforgiveness will spawn bitterness.

Bitterness stems from offenses, either real or perceived, that we hold inside ourselves. It makes us want to see the other person hurt as much as he or she hurt us. It poisons our feelings and keeps us from being able to see positive changes in others.

Malcolm contacted Tim for help after his wife, Sharon, left him. He had been emotionally neglecting her for years, and she reached the point of being fed up. Her departure snapped Malcolm into an awareness of what he had been doing, and he started working on his problems. Six months later Tim contacted Sharon to ask her to come in to the office. She came reluctantly. In the session she said, "I can't forgive Malcolm for all the years of hurt. I know it's not right, but I just don't want to let go of my anger. If I let go, it feels like I'm letting him off the hook. Besides, he hasn't changed a bit. He's still the same person as when

I left." The fact of the matter was, however, that Malcolm had changed significantly. Sharon could not or did not want to see the growth because she was looking through eyes clouded with bitterness. By holding on to her anger, understandably, she was trying to keep safe. She didn't want to trust Malcolm with her feelings and get hurt again. Forgiving someone *is* risky business.

Resolving Bitterness

In our research we found very little on the subject of forgiveness. The reason may be that outside of Christ's teachings there really is no solution to bitterness. According to the world's system it doesn't make much sense to forgive. It is only by faith in Jesus Christ and by using the power of the Holy Spirit that we can be healed of the deep roots of bitterness, one of the most destructive emotions a person can experience.

Bitterness, when left unchecked, can cause serious physical, emotional, and spiritual problems: "looking diligently lest anyone fall short of the grace of God; lest any root of bitterness springing up cause trouble, and by this many become defiled" (Heb. 12:15). Medical experts assert that a significant percentage of illness in Americans is caused by psychological and emotional factors rather than by physiological factors.

The irony of bitterness and resentment is that it winds up hurting the bitter person the most! Not only can it cause serious physical problems, but also it affects us spiritually and emotionally. Scripture teaches that unforgiveness is the one poison that will hinder our progress and prevent God from giving us full forgiveness: "For if you forgive men their trespasses, your heavenly Father will also forgive you. But if you do not forgive men their trespasses, neither will your Father forgive your trespasses" (Matt. 6:14–15). Consider the following to help to resolve bitterness.

A. *Stop feeding your bitterness.*

Our memory is a wonderful gift from the Lord; with it we recall all the warm and wonderful happenings of life. We also remember and learn from past mistakes. Unfortunately, we can also turn our memory into an ally for bitterness. Our mind has an incredible ability to remember and rehash offenses. Psychotherapists tell us that people cling to their bitterness to the bitter end. It's one of the most difficult problems to deal with.

However, you can choose to rid yourself of bitterness if you really desire to. The first step is to *stop feeding it*. When you are tempted again to dwell on the offense, to dredge up the ugly past, to feel the resentment and to feed on the hate, choose instead to starve your bitterness by refusing to relive all the old hurts. Substitute your thought patterns with positive thoughts about other people whom you love and respect.

Although you may not be able to forget your bitterness instantly, you can recognize that it is not the whole of your world. View this experience as an opportunity to learn patience, forgiveness, and a new depth of love. Recognize that God gave *everything* to you to reconcile you and restore you. Scripture tells us that we deserved death but have been wonderfully pardoned by God. Can we do less for those who have sinned against us?

B. *Stop keeping score.*

Bitterness quickly becomes exaggerated when we begin to keep score and pile up new perceived offenses and incidents. Our "lawyer" minds shout to build a case. Soon *everything* this person does starts to be offensive to us! We become super-sensitized to any perceived threats, and we distort what other people are saying or doing.

This was the case for Ramona, a client of Tim's. Hurt repeatedly in relationships with men, she no longer trusted men in general. When a man that she was seriously dating didn't call her when he said he would, she immediately pulled back and became "unavailable." When she described this to Tim he drew an analogy to help her see how she was overreacting. He said:

"It's as if you have been in charge of a radar station on the North Pole. The enemy has already launched a successful bombing attack, and your country has been seriously hurt. In order to make sure that that never happens again, you have decided to turn up your radar to full blast. Before a real bomber gets anywhere close, your highly sensitive radar picks up the signal. Unfortunately, you have it turned up so high that whenever a bird flies overhead it looks to you like a B-52. Unless you turn it down you will be constantly overreacting."

C. *Stop justifying your bitter feelings.*

The human psyche can come up with very elaborate excuses for hanging on to bitterness. That is because we want to hang on to it! Recognize that God offers no excuse for harboring bitterness, resentment, or unforgiveness. Simply put, we *must forgive:* The Christian has no option.

Overcoming Bitterness

Part of the risk of *loving greatly* is being *hurt greatly*. If we didn't care so much in the first place, we wouldn't hurt so much. Bitterness is often love gone sour.

In our human relationships, we need to learn to love with an open-ended kind of love—the same kind of love that God showed us when He sent Jesus, His precious Gift, to the world. If our love is not received or is misunderstood, we must *redirect it*—keep sending, keep loving. Otherwise we become shriveled and atrophied.

Once you've thought through these ideas, you can take some positive steps to overcoming bitterness.

A. *Start forgiving.*

Whereas nothing is more harmful to us than bitterness and unforgiveness, nothing is more liberating than forgiveness. Forgiveness is a gift that God has given us so that we can give it to others. In so doing we give it back to ourselves. Forgiveness is a choice as well as a process. We begin the process when we decide to forgive another, but it usually takes a number of repeated choices to keep that process alive. The initial choice to forgive is usually the hardest, though the results are well worth the risk. Forgiveness will result in a reduction of tension and stress, a better chance to be healthy, and an inner peace and joy.

B. *Start turning your resentment into kindness.*

Jesus gave the instruction to "love your enemies, bless those who curse you, do good to those who hate you" (Matt. 5:44). Psychologists confirm this principle, telling us that an important step to health is *acting out* our beliefs to *strengthen* them.

One of the most powerful ways to do this is to pray for another person. When we are asking God to bless another (even if that person doesn't deserve it!), we are actually loving that person in an active, powerful way. This act of submission to God also helps us feel more in control of our own life.

C. *Start giving your feelings to God.*

With God's help you can overcome bitterness. Every time you are tempted to dwell on your bitterness, give it over to God.

A helpful mental picture to substitute for negative images is to imagine yourself stuffing all your bitter feelings into a big sack (use as many sacks as it takes). Then picture yourself dumping this sack into a bottomless pit in front of the cross of Christ. We are told that God removes our sins as far away from us as the "east is from the west" (Ps. 103:12). Ask God to restore to you remembrances of positive times with the person who has hurt you, as well as memories of positive qualities.

The first thing we must assess in any strained or broken relationship is that relationship's worth. We must try to filter through our feelings of hurt and betrayal to realize that intimate relationships are hard to come by. Think of the hours and days of intimate building that have taken place between you and your spouse. Remember that Jesus was betrayed, and He did not forsake, castigate, or write off those who betrayed Him.

Remember Rachel? She began to assess what her marriage was worth. Was the offense worth giving up the marriage? She decided that in spite of being deeply hurt by Dave, she still did love him, and that although the road back was difficult, the marriage was worth the effort. She knew that to have any peace she must extend forgiveness.

You must initiate (regardless of who is at fault) the extension of forgiveness. Go the second, the third mile. Yes, that means a willingness to swallow pride and hurt, to put your trust and emotions back out in the open where they risk being hurt again.

An unknown author wrote:

To love at all is to be vulnerable. Love anything and your heart will certainly be wronged and possibly be broken. If you want to make sure of keeping it intact, you must give your heart to no one. Wrap it carefully with baubles and little luxuries, avoid all entanglements, lock it safe in a casket of your own selfishness. There it will not be broken. It will become unbreakable, impenetrable, irredeemable.[1]

Whatever it takes, give and receive forgiveness so that you can be released to laugh, love, and grow again. When people are jammed up with negative emotion, such as unforgiveness, effective problem solving becomes much more difficult. That's why we've talked about forgiveness first. When you've released your bitterness you're more capable of moving on to practical problem solving by setting goals.

2. SETTING GOALS

In Chapter 14 we gave you some ideas on how to begin self-nurturing. We told you that there are five basic areas of our personhood: emotional, mental, social, spiritual, and physical. We asked you to take out five sheets of paper and write one of these headings at the top of each page. Underneath each heading, we suggested you list appropriate activities.

Dorothy, a woman we counseled, listed, "I want to go back to college to finish my degree." "But," she told us, "I could never have the time to do that now." We suggested she start by taking one or two classes. She felt she didn't have enough time to do that either. We then suggested that she buy the textbook of one class and begin by reading it. "That," she said with a twinkle, "is within my reach."

If you only have general, long-range wishes, you will never see your goals come to pass.

It is helpful if you break your long-range goals into smaller components. That way, it's easier to realize that you can begin your journey toward them now. You can accomplish this by writing down the long-range goal.

Dorothy's long-range goal was actually to become a high-school English teacher. "When my youngest child, who's three, enters junior high, I'd like to be ready to teach," she said.

We pointed out to Dorothy that she had about nine years before her three-year-old would be in junior high, and that if she broke her long-range goal into small components it was achievable. Dorothy discovered that not only could she begin by reading a textbook each quarter while her toddler demanded constant care but that the local university would allow her to take the course final exam. If she passed, they'd give her credit for the course! In addition, the department head said he would give her eight units of credit for what he called "life experience." She also realized that in two years she could take classes in her major that were available while her child was at kindergarten. Suddenly an *impossible* dream for Dorothy had become a realistic and achievable goal, and her attitude, even toward her husband and family, seemed to be renewed.

Write your goal down, and then break it into smaller components. Research how it can be accomplished. Be creative in finding ways around the obvious obstacles. Above all, don't give up. Keep working toward the goal, piece by little piece.

3. TAKING LIFE IN PHASES

Barbara had always been told that she was somehow special, a member of an elite group of go-getters who would make it to the top of whatever field she pursued, and she believed the prediction. After all, only the cream of the crop get into Harvard University. Surrounded there by goal-oriented, aggressive students, she got caught up in a frantic passion to excel. She graduated with honors and entered the banking business.

Five years and three promotions later, Barbara left her job to have a baby. Her plan was to stay home while her children were young and return to her career later. Actually she discovered she loved being a full-time mother and homemaker. But before her first baby was crawling, Barbara began to feel guilty and uneasy about her decisions. All her friends with children worked full time. "Life shouldn't be this easy," she told herself. "I'm not producing enough. I'm not making any money. I'm not worth anything."

Barbara suffered from the temptation to want all of life *now*. In addition to setting goals, it is important to remember that we can only be one person, which is especially important for women today. Paul Tournier, in *The Gift of Feeling*, stated:

The fact is that women want both marriage and motherhood, to love, feed and care for their little intimate world, to have it to themselves, and at the same time to escape from its narrow limits, to open doors and windows on the world outside and share in the living community. It is scarcely ever really possible to reconcile these two desires; one or the other must be repressed. But the day comes when malaise, boredom, or more consciously, nostalgia, manifest themselves. Such inner conflicts give rise to feelings of frustration and guilt. The woman in the home has a bad conscience about not using the talents she has been endowed with, while the working mother worries about neglecting her children. Similarly, the spinster envies the married woman's happy family life, while the latter envies the single woman's liberty. The most truly free of all is perhaps the nun, bound by her vows!

The modern woman has plenty of models before her, and she cannot follow any of them without the risk of hankering after the privileges attaching to another. Life is indeed full of difficult choices: to live is to choose and to choose is always to renounce something—for a man as well as for a woman.[2]

Not all choices are *forever* choices. This is what we mean by the phrase *taking life in phases*. For example, you may choose to stay home with your infant child now, but plan to enter the work force again when your child starts school.

Most women do not realize that men frequently take life in phases. Some men spend twenty years in the military, retire on a pension, and start a new job. Others go to work for a company and dream of branching out or starting their own business. Often men wind up in a business or career they never intended to pursue until the opportunity came along.

Women need to see their lives in phases too. Some choices should be viewed as *forever* choices, especially for Christians. Marriage and our commitment to Christ are two examples. But viewing all of our choices as *forever* choices can overwhelm us and make us feel stifled or trapped.

Staying home and being a homemaker can be one of those choices that is not necessarily a *forever* choice. One woman told us that viewing her life in phases really helped her to enjoy, rather than resent, her current situation of "three kids under five, two still in diapers." It helped her to see that her life would not be this way forever. Life is filled with phases. We never stay where we are. Change is inevitable. And if you plan for change, the present can be much more enjoyable.

Once Barbara began to see that staying home with her child was what she wanted to do at this stage, she was more able to fully savor each day with her child, rather than view the child as a roadblock to her resuming her career in the banking business. Knowing that she planned to re-enter the work force when her child entered school, she tried to cherish each day. In the meantime she kept up with her field of expertise by reading, attending seminars, and working as a consultant on a limited basis. Although she looked forward to the future phases of her life, she also was enjoying the present.

Implementing these strategies will not always turn things around instantly. Sometimes there are irreversible limitations and handicaps, and we must learn to live with them. But if people like Joni Erickson, a paraplegic who has become an accomplished artist and public speaker, can live a full life, so can you. It happens when we begin to take steps, even small steps, toward opportunity.

CHAPTER FOURTEEN

COMMUNICATION: THE DOOR
TO INTIMACY

*G*eri was puzzled. She and Bob had been married for five years and she was wondering if the "invasion of the body snatchers" had happened to her husband. When they were courting, Bob had been spontaneous and attentive. She had loved the times of deep sharing of hopes, dreams, fears, and feelings. After they were married, their long talks became five-minute "quickies"— more an exchange of information than deep dialogue. When Geri confronted him, he said she was just being too sensitive. He loved her just as much as before; it was just that he was working hard and was physically tired.

One day Bob interrupted Geri to ask, "Where's the *TV Guide?*" while Geri was telling him about her feelings regarding her mother's phone call. Suddenly Geri burst into tears and said, "That does it Bob. The *TV Guide* is more important to you than I am." Bob sat there stunned but said nothing.

Have you ever experienced a communication frustration similar to Geri's? Chances are you have.

Nearly all of the women in our survey said things like, "I wish he could share his true feelings with me" or "I wish he would open up." Lack of communication was the single most common frustration expressed by the women we surveyed.

Women and men are often on two different levels when it comes to communicating. Women, with their training to be expressive, feel stifled by the male logical/argumentative style. Men, with their training to be rational, feel confused and a bit intimidated by the emotional expressiveness of women. As a result, men and women polarize and become frustrated in their attempts to communicate. This results in the feeling, "She/He just doesn't understand me."

A study done by Ray Birdwhistle showed that the average couple spends about 27½ minutes per week in conversation with each other. This 27½ minutes included dialogue about task-oriented as well as personal matters.¹ Most couples can change those statistics with a little effort.

To begin, here are some very helpful questions to ask yourself about your communication patterns. Ponder each of these questions and try to answer them as honestly as possible.

1. Are my communications to my partner: (A) attempts to share myself for the good of the relationship? or (B) often complaints?

2. Am I: (A) working to hear clearly what my partner is trying to communicate? or (B) self-indulgent in my communications—seeking mainly to be heard?

3. Do I talk: (A) more about how I would like to see things become or (B) more about my dissatisfactions?

4. Do I: (A) read my partner's nonverbal, as well as verbal, signals? or (B) stay absorbed in my own feelings?

5. Are my communications: (A) free of manipulation? or (B) intended to trigger a certain response?

6. Do I: (A) allow my partner space when he needs it? or (B) attempt to force communication and pressure him with questions?

7. Do I: (A) allow my partner to say his complete message? or (B) interrupt frequently?

8. Do I: (A) maintain his confidences at all costs? or (B) violate his privacy by telling others what he has told me in confidence?

9. Have I: (A) exposed my own weaknesses, needs, and tender areas? or (B) kept my walls up at all times?

10. Do I: (A) accept what he tells me without judging it? or am I (B) judgmental and prone to give advice?

Wherever you've circled (B) you are using a negative communication approach. It will be more helpful if you can adopt the positive approach in the (A) part of the question.

The important thing to remember about improving communication is to do a self-evaluation rather than focusing on your spouse. If you thought about each of the above questions, you no doubt already have some insights into improving your communication.

All expression of feeling is not productive or in the best interests of the relationship. The *motivation* behind the self-expression is the key. Are you expressing yourself to manipulate the other or to share yourself? Emotional blackmail, bullying, whining, and guilt-induction are not healthy forms of expression.

When we communicate ourself to the other ineffectively and stay stuck in the communication patterns we have used unsuccessfully for ages, the other person tends to click into the "I've heard this a million times before" mode of listening (actually nonlistening) and will ignore the message we want them so desperately to understand.

Let's take a closer look at ways we can change or improve our communication patterns.

1. SEND STRAIGHTFORWARD MESSAGES

When Ben and Natalie moved to Colorado, they purchased a fish market and began running it together. After six months or so, Natalie realized that being a shopkeeper was not what she wanted to do with the rest of her life. Her love was designing and sewing dresses, including ornate wedding gowns. And besides that, being around Ben ten hours a day was getting on her nerves.

Her husband, on the other hand, was delighted with their joint venture. He liked working with his wife and told their customers that he'd discovered paradise in a job. Natalie feared that if she told Ben how *she* really felt about their business, he'd take it personally. Meanwhile, Ben was concerned about his wife. He blamed it on long hours and little exercise, but Natalie looked and acted tired all the time. She was even starting to gain weight. Nevertheless, Ben said nothing.

Ben and Natalie were headed for a blowup. A relationship in which two people, especially a husband and wife, do not share their feelings and opinions openly cannot adapt to change or survive pressure. Nor can it allow for the expression of individuality.

But what was Natalie to do? Obviously telling Ben that she couldn't stand looking at him all day would not have been Natalie's best strategy. Keeping quiet was certainly not working. By avoiding the subject, Natalie was not being herself, which explained her frustration and moodiness.

Natalie needed to tell Ben the truth about how she felt, in a loving but straightforward manner: "Ben, I know that you really enjoy the fish market, and I'm very proud of the way you've established this business. It has also been a learning experience for me to work side by side with you these past months.

"But I have to be honest with you in telling you that my first love is designing and sewing dresses, and since we've started the store I've had no time to pursue what I most enjoy. I'd like you to consider hiring a helper so that I can phase out and go back to sewing." With this approach, Natalie would be using both tact and discretion in her communication to Ben.

2. GUARD AGAINST BEING MANIPULATIVE

In contrast to straightforward messages, we often use another type of message called manipulative communication. We learn this technique very young. Every child knows that what Mom doesn't know won't hurt her. And all of us learn to manipulate other individuals by saying what we think they want to hear. In short, we play a lot of communication games. Over a lifetime, we begin to believe that saying what we feel is not always to our advantage. And the more we shroud our true thoughts and opinions, the more we lose sight of who we really are.

Often, when women feel frustrated in their attempts to be heard by their partners, they will resort to manipulative communication techniques. One woman told Tim: "I hate to admit this, but as I've listened to myself interacting with my husband, I've become aware of the manipulations I've been using on him. I didn't realize how much I was using pouting, 'the cold shoulder,' and sarcasm to get my point across. It's going to be scary giving up those tactics, but I'm tired of sending underground messages."

Playing games with words can be destructive to both of you.

"He won't talk, so I'll also give *him* the silent treatment." "He said a cutting remark to me, so I'll say a cutting remark to him." "He put me down, so I'll find fault with him." "If he wants it, he'll have to beg."

Another manipulative tactic is a nonstop verbal assault, which rarely works on a man. When the man is reluctant to open up, the woman will often pump harder. The more silent a man is, the more the woman will talk. The more she talks, the more he will be silent. A no-win vicious cycle ensues.

Remember, men often do not feel as comfortable verbalizing their feelings as women do. The language of feeling is learned. In the typical socialization process women are taught to converse in this language and men are not. When confronted with situations requiring the skill of expressing feelings, men tend to feel unschooled and insecure. Introspection, the ability to look inward and to put one's feelings and thoughts into words, is a closely aligned skill. Like the language of feeling, it, too, is learned.

Men often use joking and teasing, not so much as true humor, but as a way to express emotion in a guarded and safe way. Rather than directly and straightforwardly expressing affection, men often resort to poking and pinching.

Manipulative types of communication from either men or women rarely produce the desired results.

3. LEARN TO BE A GOOD LISTENER

One of the most important ingredients in effective communication is listening, which is a great catalyst for helping others to open up. When you listen to and value what another person has to say, you are recognizing their worth. Listening means becoming involved in their lives. We are saying, "I may not agree with you, but I am willing to see things through your eyes." Every time we empathize with another person we are submitting to them. There is something very powerful about this kind of behavior, partly because once a person feels as if another person really wants to understand, it motivates them to want to understand the other person. If you want to be understood by your partner, then put energy into understanding your partner.

4. LEARN TO CONFRONT THOSE YOU LOVE

Another important ingredient of intimate communication is confrontation. Expressing your needs, feelings, and hurts to your partner is a necessary part of love. You are not helping anyone by playing the martyr and swallowing your confrontations. People must be real to have healthy relationships. Unexpressed feelings accumulate and begin to rule our inner lives. When negative feelings are stockpiled, they slowly, but inexorably, poison our relationships.

Women, in their assigned role as the support system to men, are given little leeway to confront. Women are trained to be supportive of men, not to threaten their egos.

If you are afraid of threatening or losing the relationship, you are not going to be in a position to risk confrontation. Often women attempt to communicate their truths in disguised ways—to send the message but to do it in such a way as to avoid upsetting the equilibrium too much. Underground messages do not work as they lack the clarity to be understood.

When Mary and Jack came into Tim's office, Mary was harboring lots of resentment because Jack was constantly putting her down. She had to learn that it was much more effective to say, "Jack, when you call me jelly-buns, I feel very hurt. Please don't *ever* do that again," instead of trying to get the message across by banging the pots and pans together as she cleaned up after dinner. When she finally did learn, however, Jack heard and responded to her request.

We all need to be held accountable for our behavior. It is an aspect of helping each other to grow. Who knows your husband's weaknesses better than you (and God), and who knows yours better than your husband? Unfortunately, when we are in a fight, we often use our insights to go for the jugular rather than to lovingly confront each other with the truth.

The prerequisite for our confronting another is self-examination—scrutinizing our own motives and hearts. This allows us to approach the other person in humility. Rather than "this is the way it is," we can have an attitude of "this is the way I see it, but I may be wrong."

If, instead, we act as if we know the "right" way, we will blame our partners for their ways, which triggers a defensive response. How often have you participated in an encounter that went something like this?

John's hammer was missing again. In his usual rising-to-a-pitch, blaming tone, he yelled from the laundry room, "Where's my hammer?!" Dottie had been through this before. "I don't know where your hammer is," she replied. By now John was half-way down the hall and moving toward her. "How many times have I told you to put it back! You never put my things where I can find them," he said.

Now Dottie was hot, "I didn't take your dumb hammer! You probably left it in the garage. Why do you always blame me— you're not so perfect yourself, buster!"

Words like *never* and *always*, spoken in accusatory tones, will nearly always project blame, and more often than not, they will start arguments.

John *could* have said, "Have you seen my hammer? I seem to have misplaced it." And Dottie *could* have responded, "Maybe it was left in the garage. I'll help you look for it." But unfortunately, most of us tend to accuse or blame first.

If you have been locked into a pattern of mutual blaming and you attempt to change your part of the pattern and to confront in a new way, you can expect that your partner's response will likely not be "I'm so glad you brought this up, and I really appreciate that you have pointed out something I need to work on," but instead defensive disqualification of what you have said. If this happens, do not lose hope and abandon your message. Ingrained patterns that have taken years to develop (and often repeat the type of exchanges we learned at a young age) do not change overnight.

When you receive a defensive reaction to your communication and your message is being discounted or contradicted, do not counterattack or withdraw your message. It is more helpful to restate yourself clearly in the context of, "You may not see it the way I do, but this is my perspective and these are my feelings. You do not have to agree with me, but allow me my view."

5. THINK BEFORE YOU SPEAK

Before you communicate your message, slow down and think out what you are trying to say. It is often helpful to bounce your thoughts and feelings off another person whom you trust, someone who is not involved in the situation and can give you objective feedback. Gather alternative points of view.

Before you go around baring your soul, check your attitude. "Let all bitterness, wrath, anger, clamor, and evil speaking be put away from you, with all malice" (Eph. 4:31). This injunction requires that you act only out of kindness and compassion and that you forgive others for the ways in which their honesty may have offended you.

If you want to communicate your feelings clearly but are fearful of being cut off before you can get your message out, you may find it helpful to write out what you want to say in a letter. This allows time to reflect and to express yourself in a positive way before you get into the heat of the moment. You may even want to give the letter to him before you talk face to face. When you do talk, remain calm. Your feelings have an important place, but they must be expressed in a modulated fashion.

6. SPEAK THE TRUTH, IN LOVE

Most people appreciate the truth, even if it hurts, but it has to be presented with the right attitude, at an appropriate time, and in the proper manner. The Bible says we are to speak the truth, but we are to do it in love (Eph. 4:15). Speaking the truth in love means that we give messages of our well-thought-out perceptions in such a way as to serve the best interests of the relationship. In other words, don't let any "corrupt communication proceed out of your mouth, but what is good for necessary edification, that it may impart grace to the hearers" (Eph. 4:29).

It requires discernment to know *what* to say to build up the other person and the relationship and *when* to say it. What we say may be a painful message to hear, but there is a great deal of difference between a message that is intended to hurt and one that is intended to heal. Prayer is vital to discernment.

7. USE "I" RATHER THAN "YOU"

Veronica and Nathan were locked into a perpetual no-win fight about his tendency to set up his recreational activities without first consulting with her about her plans. Veronica would respond by saying, "You are so selfish—you act just like a little kid." Of course, he reacted defensively and usually, at this point, stalked off. Veronica was acting parental, and she hooked into the rebellious child in Nathan. The pattern became so established that she only needed to sound slightly parental about his recreational plans to get the same response. Veronica found that Nathan reacted much more positively to the message, "It may be my hang-up but this is really important to me. I need to know about your plans so I can coordinate schedules with you." Notice that she avoided any judgment about his behavior. Instead she made a clear request regarding her need. When you communicate your message, make sure you communicate an "I" message and not a "you" message.

An "I" message usually has three components: feeling, behavior, and impact (FBI for short). It consists of: I feel __(feeling)__ when __(behavior)__ because __(impact)__. For example, "I feel frustrated when you are late for dinner and do not call to let me know beforehand, because I time the dinner to be done at 7:00 and it gets dried out and cold by 8:00." "I" messages avoid blame and help us to take responsibility for our own perspectives. They also lead to problem solving and help us to get off the merry-go-round of accusations. "I" messages are received better by the hearer too.

Here's another example. Instead of saying, "You never spend any time with me anymore," it is much more productive to say, "I feel lonely much of the time, and I would like to have some one-to-one time with you each day, even if it's only for ten minutes."

Men, with their orientation to problem solving, are much more likely to listen to you if you talk about the specifics of the problem and look for solutions. Express your emotions in the context of what you want instead of what you don't like.

8. LEARN THE ART OF FAIR FIGHTING

There is a place in a healthy relationship for the constructive kind of mutual confrontation some have called fair fighting. Fair fighting is the interaction two people have when they level with each other with regard to an issue about which they are in disagreement and have strong feelings. We are told in Ephesians 4:26 to "Be angry, and do not sin: do not let the sun go down on your wrath." In the Greek text the first part of the verse is a double imperative. Each section contains equal weight. We have often distorted it to read "*If* you are angry, don't sin." The true meaning can be paraphrased, "It is imperative that you be angry and it is imperative that you not sin." In other words, be what you are. If you are angry, don't try to cover it up. It is also important that you choose an expression of anger that is loving—both to yourself and to the one with whom you are angry. When we let the sun go down on our anger, we leave room for ourselves to express it in some distorted, underground form.

Intimate partners have fights, but their fights are constructive and clear the air. Their fights also equalize the partners and bond them together so one is not strong and the other weak.

Some ground rules facilitate fair fighting.

A. Do not use name calling or character assassination. Avoid labels: they push people into corners and make people defensive.

B. Keep to the issue. Remember what you are fighting about and get to the bottom line. Do not "throw in the kitchen sink."

C. Be specific. Describe exactly what you are thinking and feeling. Your goal is to help the other person understand you— not to conquer with a mass of words.

D. Ask for a certain change. Let your partner know exactly what you are after.

E. Work at being open and vulnerable. It's hard in the heat of the moment to drop the shield, but candid disclosure can cut through a stalemate to bring a solution.

F. Give feedback to your partner. Reflect back to him what you hear him saying, and check out if that is what he wants to communicate. Do not try to read his mind.

G. Don't bring up the past. Old wounds may be on your mind, but their insertion into the here-and-now will muddy the water.

H. Consider a compromise. Perhaps there is a way that you

both can "win" though it may take the form of something that is not exactly the way each of you would like.[2]

Keep your focus on resolving the conflict rather than on winning. The aim of an argument is to overpower the other. The aim of communication is to strengthen the bond of intimacy. One psychologist, Ari Kiev, drew a practical analogy about arguing: "Think of yourselves as being together in the same canoe. When you start escalating the argument, you're both standing up in the canoe and you're both going to fall in the water together. When the realization sinks in, most people start thinking less about themselves and more about the canoe."[3]

Above all, remember that your dialogue with your partner is to be an honest search for God's will for your relationship.

9. TALK ABOUT SEX

One of the greatest communication breakdowns between husbands and wives is in the area of their sexual relationship. Because it is such a tender issue for both, it is usually very difficult for couples to be open and vulnerable. As a result, misunderstanding (and the subsequent hurt feelings) is plentiful.

In the movie *Annie Hall*, when a psychiatrist asked Woody Allen, "How often do you have sex?" he replied, "Hardly ever—three times a week." When the psychiatrist asked Annie Hall the same question, she replied, "All the time, three times a week." Men often seek to express their feelings of love through sex when they feel inadequate or afraid of expressing those feelings verbally. It is common for a man who is trying to make up with his wife after an argument to head her back to the bedroom. One frustrated woman told Tim, "I wish he would stop trying to patch everything up by going to bed. When I want to talk about my hurt all he wants to do is make love, and I feel used." Often women will desire to be held and cuddled and nothing more, but men typically read this as a sexual come-on. The communication lines get garbled, and if she gives in she feels resentful. If she backs off, he feels hurt. The way out of this tangle is to start to give each other clear messages about your thoughts and feelings regarding your sexual relationship. It is certainly risky, but it can resolve much pain.

10. BE PATIENT

If you find that your mate seems indifferent or resistant to your attempts to deepen the level of communication in your relationship, it is essential that you drop any attempts to force him to open up. Instead, work to create an atmosphere of safety. When he does open up, respect his thoughts and feelings. Maintain his privacy. Reinforce his efforts to communicate. The early attempts are like tender sprouts: They are fragile and need to be treated with care. Praise acts as nourishment to strengthen the new growth. Let him know how much you value being close to him. Create new experiences to be together. Find new ways to express affection. Talk about your dreams and fears, and reminisce about previously shared times of closeness. Do not take his problems with opening up as a personal rejection, but allow him to struggle. There are also times in your relationship when it will be necessary to have "spaces in your togetherness." Take time-outs to refuel.

In the next chapter we will address the general topic of how to develop intimacy. A grasp of the principles of healthy communication will give you a solid base from which to develop closeness with your partner.

CHAPTER FIFTEEN

THE ART OF INTIMACY

Among intelligent People
The surest basis for marriage
is Friendship,
the Sharing of real interests,
the ability to fight out
ideas together
and understand each other's
thoughts and dreams.

Kahlil Gibran, Beloved Prophets*

*W*hen Jan and Steve were courting, they couldn't spend *enough* time with each other. Candlelight dinners, long walks on the beach, and window shopping trips together were the rule— not the exception. In fact, when they weren't together physically, they made sure to call each other at least once a day.

After they had been married three wonderful years, their first child was born. Until then, life was rather predictable. Both worked; neither traveled. Both went home at six o'clock; neither worked on weekends. Both shared household chores; neither complained. Then baby Jessie arrived.

Afterward Steve traveled and Jan worked weekends. What little time they had together, they tried to spend with Jessie, but something was very, very wrong. They had no time alone for talking, much less lovemaking. Jan was convinced that they were drifting apart. Steve was sure that Jan loved the baby more than she loved him. Unwilling to compete for attention, he retreated into the loving arms of his job. Jan looked more and more to Jessie to provide the emotional strokes she craved.

*Virginia Hite, ed., *Beloved Prophets: The Love Letters of Kahlil Gibran and Mary Haskell* (New York: Alfred A. Knopf, 1972), 408.

When Jan and Steve finally sat down together for a long talk, both were puzzled. What had happened to the closeness they once shared?

Perhaps you can identify with their problem. Jan and Steve's circumstances demonstrate how jealousy, insecurity, and distance can creep into a relationship almost *naturally*. As A. W. Tozer wrote, "The bent of nature is toward the wild, not toward the fruitful field." In other words, leave the garden unattended, and the weeds will take over. In a marriage, if you do what comes naturally—what's routine and comfortable—your relationship will deteriorate, and you'll drift apart. *Intimacy takes work.*

Jan was right; she and Steve were drifting apart. And perhaps Steve was even on track when he began to feel as if he played second fiddle to the baby. It happens all the time. The wife feels neglected, so she pours all her love and affection into her children. But Steve never told Jan how he felt. And Jan never shared her uneasiness. So who's to blame? Both, of course.

At this point you may be wondering what intimacy entails. Intimates:

- Trust each other. There is an atmosphere of safety that allows partners to be open and vulnerable.
- Share control of the relationship with each other. No one person dominates with his or her will.
- Allow each other to be individuals. They respect each other's privacy and provide emotional space.
- Are dedicated to each other's growth. Each makes the other top priority.
- Welcome expression of the partner's "free child." They know how to laugh and play with each other.
- Are able to conflict with each other in a healthy way. Conflict brings them closer to each other.

At this point you may be saying to yourself, "I'd love to develop this type of closeness with my husband, but I don't think he will respond."

DO MEN WANT INTIMACY?

The simple fact remains that men in our culture generally have trouble making connection with their feelings and emotions. It's just not the "manly" thing to do. Every time a man shares his feelings, he risks rejection, scorn, and misunderstanding, as does a woman. But for the man, loss of power and self-control can be too great a price to pay for venting his emotions. So he selects his listeners carefully or chooses not to talk at all.

But does this mean that men are not interested in true intimacy? Hardly. Peter Marin, writer in *Psychology Today,* reported a survey in which he found that "the commercialization of sex destroys true feelings."[1]

What struck us about Marin's survey of contemporary sexual attitudes was his frank repudiation of a commonly accepted assumption that the man's sex drive is the most important compulsion in his life, a "primary source of pleasure for everyone."[2] He asked the reader to listen carefully to what moved beneath people's words. He concluded:

> The loneliness and dissatisfaction that most people express, the yearnings they articulate, have much less to do with sex than with an unfulfilled desire for good company or good conversation or the intimacy of shared perceptions and interests. I would say that friendship and community seem more important to most people. . . . What seems to dominate their concerns about sex when they do surface is a sort of idealized and sugary notion, brought up to date with erotic trimmings—a child's drawing of security extended to include sex: A house with smoke curling from the chimney, a couple hand-in-hand at the door, and behind them, upstairs, the circular mirrored bed into which, after the day's work has been done and the front and back doors locked, they tumble for a riotous good time.[3]

We think Marin is saying, in no uncertain terms, that the yearning for intimacy, for companionship, is one of man's greatest motivators. It's not conquest, and it's not sexual power, but it's the desire for love. If this is true, then it is important for you to know because it means that behind your husband's facade there is hope for the intimacy you desire.

This is one issue that can make or break a relationship. If, as a woman, you assume that men have one thing on their minds and one thing only, you'll have a hard time trusting any man. But if you can listen beneath a man's words, as Marin suggests, you might find something totally unexpected.

Consider the implications of the research of Lois Leiderman Davitz, Ph.D., author of *Living in Sync: Men and Women in Love.* She surveyed four hundred divorced men between the ages of twenty and forty-five for *McCall's.* In an article entitled "Why Men Divorce," she revealed some surprising contradictions to popular myths about why marriages fail. "What virtually every man in our study cited as decisive to the failure of the relationship was the *lack of companionship.* Universally, these men felt that their marriages fell apart because they stopped being friends with their wives."[4]

And how did these men define companionship? A companion, they said, is someone with whom you share activities that you enjoy. "It's not sex, though a desire for sex may grow out of companionship. It's not parallel activities such as sitting together and watching T.V. It's not necessarily outings with their children."[5]

Davitz sees a man's desire for female companionship as a shift in his expectations. "In the past," she says, "men often turned to other men for companionship, but today, they'd rather spend time with their wives." Unfortunately, this shift comes at a time when many women are feeling overwhelmed by their multiple roles as wage earners, home managers, wives, and mothers. Wrote Davitz: "As women struggle to meet expanded challenges, there's a very real danger that the men they love are being squeezed out of their lives."[6]

It is also clear from the *McCall's* survey that men and women define communication in totally different ways. Most men don't care much for sitting down to talk about their most intimate feelings. They find such conversations mechanical and uncomfortable and would much prefer to share their feelings as a byproduct of another activity. In other words, they tend to express their feelings when they are engaged in the kinds of activities they do with companions. Thus your husband may be desiring a safer variation of intimacy—companionship—whereas you may be searching for a deep level of emotional closeness.

SPENDING TIME TOGETHER

Spending a great deal of time together does not guarantee an intimate marriage. For intimacy to flourish, however, spending time together is a necessary prelude. The sharing of experiences bonds people together. Experiences give you something to talk about and may lead to deeper sharing. Intimacy is often a product of habit and a gradual lowering of the protective walls we keep between us. When we share life together, our bonds are strengthened.

Tim and his wife, Anita, met at a summer camp where they were counselors for mentally and physically handicapped children. "The initial glow of our romance was soon tempered by the reality of feeding, bathing, dressing, and transporting a cabin full of kids," Tim remembers. "We saw each other at our 'worst'— short-tempered, impatient, clumsy, and in an embarassing situation at least once a day. We found, however, that our relationship, stripped of the pretense of dating, grew solid and matured. The experiences that we shared that summer became a foundation of our emotional bonding. We still love to get out the scrapbook and laugh about those camp days."

LEARNING TO ENJOY EACH OTHER'S HOBBIES

Another way of getting closer to your husband is to get involved with something he loves. This may take some doing.

In a counseling session in Tim's office, Sandra was dealing with the impact of the differences between her husband and her. "For instance," she said, "Victor was so excited about the football game he was watching on Sunday and tried to explain to me how important the game was. To me it was just a game like all the hundreds of games he watches. If my son or someone I knew played on the team, I could understand." For Tim, it was easy to identify with Victor's excitement. He did have a type of relationship with his team. He identified closely with them on the field and received vicarious satisfaction from their accomplishments.

You do not have to love the activity he enjoys, but you may be able simply to enjoy his enthusiasm. Sharing in each other's emotions will bond you together.

SHARING IN EACH OTHER'S CAREERS

It's important to share in each other's careers, whether it's an office or at-home career. We do not have to understand the complexities of each other's jobs, but we should try to share some of our work experiences. Sometimes we tend to feel that we have to have something exciting to tell about our day, but simply relating our feelings about the day, even if it was the same old routine, can be helpful.

PRAYING TOGETHER

Praying together is a shared experience that has a great potential to build intimacy. Many men find, however, that praying in a group is actually easier than one-to-one with their wives, so they shy away from doing it. You can do a number of things to help him overcome his fear.

Try writing your prayers and exchanging them. Ask your husband if there's a specific thing you can pray for in your private prayer time. If you have special prayer needs, simply ask, "Will you pray with me about. . . ?" Don't forget to share praises, answers to prayer, and perhaps a personal spiritual victory.

TAKING TIME TO BE ALONE TOGETHER

When was the last time you and your husband spent any significant amount of time alone together? If you are typical, those times come few and far between, especially if you have children at home. Healthy marriages require time alone together. There is something very powerful about deliberately looking into your partner's eyes and touching them in a way that says, "Right now, you are the center of my attention."

One couple that followed through on Tim's recommendation to get away for a weekend came back and reported that they had to go through an initial adjustment period on their trip. They were so unused to being alone that they didn't know how to relate without the kids in the back seat.

If you haven't spent much private time with your mate lately, consider setting up a weekend interlude (without the kids—of course).

MODELING INTIMACY

Men often get stuck in their fears of getting close, or they feel inadequate to know how to do it.

How can a man, who has not learned the skills involved in emotional closeness, change? By watching you become open and vulnerable.

Joyce was extremely frustrated with Walter. He loved their son, Tommy, but had a great deal of difficulty understanding the child's problems. One day when Tommy came home from school crying about being picked on by the school bully, Walter told Tommy to stop whining and being a sissy. Rather than stepping in as Tommy's rescuer, Joyce waited until later to talk with Walter.

"I remember when I was a kid and the other girls picked on me. I used to feel so helpless," she told him. By doing this she helped Walter form an emotional link with his own past. Later he went up to Tommy and related how he too had been picked on by the class bully. Walter and Tommy's relationship took a giant leap forward. Joyce modeled an ingredient of intimacy, and Walter picked up on it.

REINFORCING HIS EFFORTS TOWARD INTIMACY

If your husband has been keeping an emotional distance but has started to respond to your efforts to facilitate intimacy, you can expect that his first steps will be shaky and tentative. Your response at this time is very important. You can either protect and feed these tender shoots, or you can squash them. It is common for women who have become bitter over the lack of intimacy in their relationships to squelch their husband's small but significant attempts to change.

Joan and Fred found themselves locked into a frustrating pattern. Both wanted closeness, but both were afraid of being the only vulnerable one. One day when Fred opened himself up to Joan, she was in her shut-down mode, and she responded to him with distance and coldness. Predictably, Fred felt rejected and pulled back emotionally. When Joan realized what was happening, she decided to give Fred a stroke for the risk he'd taken. She said, "Fred, I can see you are really trying to reach out and I appreciate it. My feelings are still tender. Please be patient with me and I'll get there." It is hard to submit in this way, especially when we are jammed up by our pride.

Here are some practical tips that you can enlist to help maintain intimacy in your marriage.

- Set up a regular, weekly date with your spouse. Put these dates on your calendar and protect them from interruptions.

- Consider budgeting money for support services that would give you more time with your spouse (i.e., send laundry to the cleaners, get cleaning help, arrange for baby sitting occasionally).

- Keep a personal calendar on which you record all your planned activities, and review it with your spouse regularly. Use it to anticipate times of stress, and plan and pray accordingly. If your priorities must be compromised from time to time, schedule make-up times for getting away with your spouse.

- Take "little moments" in the day—a shared cup of tea, a walk, a backrub—things that are relaxing.

- Get away together as often as possible, even if it's just for a night at a local hotel. Recognize that your husband may not realize that a temperature reading of your relationship is in order. One woman said that her husband never knew he was hungry until she put food in front of him. Many men don't sense their hunger for intimacy until they get a taste of it.

- Laugh and play together. Allow your "free child" to come out.

- Kidnap your husband from time to time. Some women show up at their husband's office around lunch time. Others plan romantic surprise dates.

- Find common ground that you both can enjoy. Choose something that does not center around your children, work, or church. This can be a hobby, sports activity, or whatever. Use your creativity!

Building intimacy takes a lot of work. It may sound as if we are setting up women to be the ones responsible for the level of intimacy of the relationship. But one person cannot make a relationship close. Intimacy requires reciprocity. One person can, however, help pave the way to intimacy. When one person makes him or herself vulnerable, the possibility of intimacy is enhanced. Maintaining an "I'm-not-going-to-open-up-until-he/she-does" attitude will keep the barriers up.

The best way to find intimacy is to be an intimate person. Instead of demanding openness and sharing, create an atmosphere of safety in your relationship that will facilitate his opening up. Give up your attempts to pry him open, but maintain the clear message that you desire to share in his life. Paving the way to intimacy in marriage is a lot like developing a deep friendship. Friendships do not spring up spontaneously. They require work and take time to cultivate.

In the next chapter we will explore some specific skills related to building a partnership.

CHAPTER SIXTEEN

LIVING THE PARTNERSHIP

Two are better than one,
Because they have a good reward for their labor.
For if they fall, one will lift up his companion.
But woe to him who is alone when he falls,
For he has no one to help him up.
Again, if two lie down together, they will keep warm;
But how can one be warm alone?
Though one may be overpowered by another,
    Two can withstand him.

    Ecclesiastes 4:9–12

One woman, when asked what is the most difficult thing for her personally about working with men, answered, "I usually have to allow them to think an idea is theirs before they will accept it."

Another woman, when responding to how she is most frequently put down, said, "Assumptions are made by men that women can't make wise decisions or are not farsighted."

Perhaps the most descriptive comment we received from our survey on this subject was, "I am made to feel like I don't have enough brains to make decisions, yet I'm the one in our family who makes sure all the bills are paid on time."

Since the turn of the century, our culture has taken two giant steps—some might call them leaps—that have had a profound effect on men/women relationships. Step One was from the farm to the suburbs. As recently as eighty years ago, most American families made their living in agriculture. Today only 3 percent operate working farms. Step Two was women's moving from the home to the work place. Women now make up nearly one-half the total work force, and for the first time in American history, more women are in the labor force than out of it. What's more, 60 percent of all married mothers with children younger than six now work outside the home.

These two steps have made a lasting imprint on values and lifestyles in America. Changes in women's career status, in particular, have altered the basic fabric of relationships between men and women, married or not. When a woman no longer needs the status of Mrs. or a man's money, the balance of power in male/female relationships shifts.

Although the balance of power may be slowly shifting toward women, the workload at home still seems to be primarily the woman's responsibility. Most of the women we surveyed said they didn't get enough help from their husbands. "I wish he understood how many 'hats' I must wear. I need more help at home. He knows this intellectually, but practically I get little help at home."

Furthermore, the basic fabric of the family has been challenged as never before. Now we have two-career marriages, in which the question of whose career is more important becomes a major issue as it relates to the well-being of the family.

Who goes with whom when job offers are in different cities? Who will care for and nurture the children? Do the children now wind up with two parents who care more about their careers than about the family? Previously, the children at least had the near total attention of one parent (mother). Now it might be reasonable to say that they have less than half the attention of both parents. In essence the family is often the second priority. No longer do we have a cohesive unit, but we have an "arrangement" that is both tense and tentative.

WORKING WOMEN—THREATENED MEN

A questionnaire completed by twenty thousand readers of *McCall's* suggested that a troubling phenomenon now exists. In an article entitled "Marriage: What Women Expect and What They Get," it was reported that the women with the greatest career involvement had the most complaints about their marriages. They were less happy with their own lives and cited stress as one of the most nagging problems.[1]

In fact, one survey of two thousand women gave the startling statistic that for every additional $1,000 earned by the wife, the divorce rate rises 2 percent for working couples.[2]

Why is this so? Could it be that career-oriented women expect more of their mates? (They've changed, so why doesn't he?) Perhaps a woman's perceptions of the ideal man, which include his demeanor and his values, change when she enters the workplace. She meets more men—more models to whom she can compare her husband. Or is it because women are looking to their jobs and the relationships they form with people on the job to meet needs their husbands have failed to meet? Or maybe the husband feels threatened by his wife's success. His role as provider (thus his self-esteem and definition of success) is threatened or, worse yet, no longer needed.

Allen Bloom, professor of philosophy at the University of Chicago, struck a resonant chord in his book, *The Closing of the American Mind.* As of this writing, the book has been on the *New York Times* best-seller list for twenty weeks. With regard to the male way of thinking in America, Bloom stated that the "souls of men—their ambitious, warlike, protective, possessive character—must be dismantled in order to liberate women from their domination." He went on to state that the "re-education process of men" is an attempt to get men to "accept the 'feminine elements' in their nature." However, as Bloom pointed out, "Men tend to undergo this re-education somewhat sullenly but studiously, in order to avoid the opprobrium of the sexist label and to keep peace with their wives and girlfriends. And it is indeed possible to soften men. But to make them 'care' is another thing, and the project must inevitably fail."[3]

Bloom contended that this failure is due in part to the man's feeling that his family is part of his property—to be protected, defended, provided for, and cared for. Said Bloom, "When wives and children come to the husband and father and say, 'We are not your property; we are ends in ourselves and demand to be treated as such,' the anonymous observer cannot help being impressed. But the difficulty comes when wives and children further demand that the man continue to care for them as before. . . ."[4]

Bloom's point is that if the husband/father, who has a strong need to protect and provide for his family, like the other property he "owns," has lost his primary motivation for being the husband/father, he will inevitably "cease being a father and become a mere man again, rather than turning into a providential God, as others ask him to be."[5]

Sarcastically Bloom stated, "Law may prescribe that the male nipples be made equal to the female ones, but they still will not give milk."[6] He continued:

> Women are pleased by their successes, their new opportunities, their agenda, their moral superiority. But underneath everything lies the more or less conscious awareness that they are still dual beings by nature, capable of doing most of the things men do and also wanting to have children. They may hope otherwise, but they fully expect to pursue careers, to have to pursue careers, while caring for children alone.[7]

Bloom's pessimism about men ever taking an equal interest and concern in the nurture of the family is based on the fact that men can opt out without too much cost. He believes that while American men are convinced of the "injustice of the old order of things," he sees the new order as primarily a woman's agenda.[8] He says that men make a rather feeble attempt at equality, but the underlying motive (i.e., This is *my* wife and *my* child and I am the man whom they need to provide and care for them) is gone.

THE RESULTS OF THESE TRENDS

So where does that leave today's working woman? Often it leaves her burning the candle at both ends. It leaves her trying to fulfill expectations and roles which carry with them a much larger agenda than ever before in history. She is driven to be a good mother, wife, and career woman. She must be competent and dedicated in her career while still being a good cook and family planner. She has to be good at both documents and diapers, cooking and commuting. She has to play the role of Miss Harvard and Mrs. Hostess at the same time. The end result is guilt, stress, burnout, and resentment.

And where does it leave the man? It leaves him frustrated,

threatened, and confused. It reinforces the vague feeling that he is no longer needed. He agrees that women have every right to pursue a career, but he now finds himself questioning his value. Often he ends up pouring more of his time into his job or hobbies and giving even less time to the family.

But is there an alternative? The traditional idea of husband-breadwinner/wife-homemaker is gone. It now represents less than 10 percent of all American households. Yet the new do-your-own-thing feminism that emphasizes the "Big I" is now found to be empty and hollow as well.

Is there middle ground where men and women can once again find true fulfillment? We think there is, but it begins with learning to work together as partners.

BUILDING A PARTNERSHIP

It is natural for you, as a woman, to want a partnership with your husband, whether or not you are a working woman. If everything else we have said in this book is true, then it stands to reason that you bring an important ingredient into the marriage. You are a vital part of the equation in making sound family decisions.

Some of you, no doubt, are already included as equal partners. Others of you wish *he* would take a greater leadership role in decision making. But the majority of you, according to our research, are not always treated as equal partners in the relationship.

This expresses itself in two distinct ways: *decision making* and *division of household labor*. In the majority of households our survey represents, women were given *less* than equal weight when making family decisions, but *more* than their share of the workload with regard to household labor. Let's discuss these two aspects as they relate to building a partnership.

Mutual Decision Making

Hal came home one day brimming with enthusiasm. He could hardly wait to sit Norma down to tell her about the great opportunity he had run across at work. A coworker, Fred, had invested in a new company that had a sure-fire scheme to make money drilling oil wells. Hal said, "Here is our chance to make enough money so I can get out of my old job, and I can start my own business."

When Norma pressed for details, Hal got irritated. "I checked everything out already," he said. When she asked if the company had a geological survey, he asked her, "When did you get your degree in geology?" Hal pressed the issue so hard that Norma backed off. And so they invested their savings in the project. Norma was angry but held in her resentment. She tried to convince herself that Hal, who normally made excellent decisions at work, probably was right. What she felt intuitively, however, but wasn't able to verbalize to herself, was that Hal was not operating on logic. Instead, he was driven from inside to prove himself. This force superseded his normal logic.

The first well was dry, and the company didn't have enough money for another. Hal and Norma lost their savings. When a sheepish Hal came home and told Norma, she had to bite her tongue to keep from saying, "I told you so."

Decision making is vitally important to any marriage. Think back over the last year of your life. Maybe you bought a new house or car, took a vacation, or made some investments, all examples of some of the bigger decisions a husband and wife make as a couple. And then there are the smaller decisions like "Should we repair the TV or buy a new one?" "Should we punish Junior for talking back or pretend we didn't hear him?" and so on.

But how should decisions be made within the marriage? One option was used by Norma and Hal. One person has the power and the other gives in. This option is fertile ground for growing resentment. In *How to Live with Another Person*, David Viscott described it this way: "A long-held secret resentment over trampled rights becomes a silent negative force seeking expression. It can flow through a relationship, attach itself to a trivial argument, make small anger great, taint what is good and angrily leak out everywhere."[9] It can also breed decisions that tend to be impulsive and not very well-rounded.

The second decision-making option is for both people to vie for control. This sets up a power struggle—an "If-you-win-then-I-lose" battle. Power is seen as something to be wrestled away from the other, and power tactics are used to gain control. This too damages the relationship.

The third option is the scriptural model of mutual submission. When a couple functions in the context of mutual submission, they make decisions together—no one person dominates with his or her will.

Many of you may greatly desire this type of partnership but, instead, find yourselves in a relationship rut. You may have already tried to break out of this rut but have discovered how hard it is to break old patterns. We would like to offer some practical steps that have the potential to help you facilitate the development of mutual decision making.

Creating a Mutual Decision-Making Pattern

1. Ask your partner to dialogue with you about how you make decisions as a couple. Help him see that part of your problem may be differing styles of decision making. It will be very helpful to get some perspective on your overall style. Remember the three styles that we've mentioned: one person dominant/one person passive; two people in a power struggle; mutual decision making. Talk together about how you can move to a mutual decision-making style.

2. If you've identified your style as dominant/passive, it is important for the passive partner to communicate his or her feelings and ideas. Before the passive partner can negotiate with the dominant partner, the passive partner must have a clear sense of his or her own beliefs, priorities, and opinions. The passive partner needs to spend some time thinking, writing, and praying about ideas. The dominant partner will be more likely to listen if he or she knows that the passive partner has reasonable, thought-out ideas than if he or she thinks the passive partner is just reacting to the dominant one's ideas.

3. If you are in a power struggle, it is vital that you realize it. A power struggle can be identified by the fact that you and your partner are resisting each other's requests—even when they are reasonable. An atmosphere of tension and anger usually acts as a smoke screen to hide a deeper fear. The way to resolve a power

struggle is to talk about the underlying fear. Often there is a fear of being controlled (I feel that if I go along with him, I will be letting him walk all over me). You can be the one to help break out of this stalemate by being the one to verbalize your fear and by letting go of the need to keep control. It is okay to surrender, to choose to let go, without a loss of self.

4. Before you attempt to do problem-solving with your partner, talk about your feelings about the particular issue. Unexpressed feelings tend to jam up the decision-making process. Closely aligned to the need to express feelings is the importance of talking about your values, beliefs, and priorities. These principles are foundational to any decisions you make, but they are often neglected. We end up talking about, "Can we afford to buy this new car?" rather than how the new car fits in with our lifestyle priorities. When we have underdeveloped priorities, we tend to make impulsive, half-baked decisions. Articulate the biblical principles involved in the issue, and integrate those into the process.

5. Many situations become clarified with the passage of time. Allow time for reflection, prayer, and mulling over the decision. Pushing and jamming in an attempt to accelerate the process leads to poor decisions and frustrated people. And remember, not all situations require a decision.

6. People come first, before the issue. Avoid pride deadlocks where you insist on your way. Defer to each other. Compromise. When one person is more affected by the decision than another, allow that person the bigger say in the outcome.

7. Set up a time to come together specifically to discuss the issue. Too many decisions between couples are made while rushing out the door in the morning. There is something very powerful about sitting across from each other at the table.

8. It is often helpful, especially when at a stalemate, to ask your partner for a written proposal (and to submit one to him). It tends to bring clarity.

When you have incorporated these principles and have developed the ability to effectively make decisions, you and your spouse will have mutual ownership of the relationship. It means that you can function as a team.

Division of Household Labor

Recently Tim overheard a conversation between his secretary and a single father. As the busy father tried to arrange a counseling appointment for his son, he said, "This is getting hectic. I don't know how I can run a business and raise two kids." You may chuckle to hear his sentiment and may even feel a sense of satisfaction. The sad fact is that women are traditionally set up to shoulder the bulk of the responsibility of taking care of home and children, and they know too well the frustration of too much to do and too little time to do it. The old cliché "A mother's work is never done" is a reality for many women.

When several advertising agencies did a survey to find out how involved husbands were in doing household chores, they found the men were more likely to talk about helping and less likely to help. One survey found that 80 percent of the men surveyed expected their wives, who worked full time, to take care of the household, shopping, and children.[10]

An interesting study done by Doyle Dane Bernback showed that 35 percent of the husbands surveyed felt that vacuuming was an acceptable chore for men. However, only 27 percent of the same men had ever done any vacuuming. The researchers concluded, "It is easier for men to accept the possibility of women as brain surgeons than to release their own wives from the drudgery of laundry and cleaning the bathroom."[11]

According to a survey done by Johnson Wax, women who work outside the home spend 11.2 hours per week doing housework; men, 3.9 hours; girls, 2.7 hours; and boys, 2.0 hours.[12]

It's a common belief that the more educated the man, the more in tune he will be to helping around the house. Not so! One study conducted by Dr. John DeFrain of the University of Nebraska, found that blue-collar men did 20 percent of the housework in their homes. In contrast, white-collar men did only 5 percent.[13]

What conclusions can we draw from the findings of these researchers? It seems clear that there is an inequitable distribution of responsibility for household/family chores in the majority of families. You can take the following steps to improve the division of labor in your home.

Improving the Division of Labor

1. The first step in opening your marriage up for change is to evaluate the current state of affairs regarding how you and your husband divide family responsibilities. How do you like the current division of labor? How does your husband feel about it? Ask him to sit down with you and dialogue about this. He may even be willing to take a quiz developed by professional cleaner Don Aslett, who dubs himself "America's cleaning guru." He has come up with a test to determine if men are pulling their weight.[14]

Men are advised to read each statement and then score themselves on a scale of 0 to 5. The scale: 0 = never; 1 = once in a while; 2 = half of the time; 3 = most of the time; and 5 = always.

Total your score at the end. If your score falls between 0 and 30, Aslett says you're a cad. Between 30 and 50, you're an underachiever. From 50 to 100 you're about average, but "nothing to brag about." Anyone who scores between 100 and 130 is a macho man. For any man who finishes with 130 to 150 points, Aslett raises his eyebrows and states unequivocally, "You're a liar."

CLEANING
_____ I tidy the house.
_____ I dust.
_____ I vacuum.
_____ I sweep or mop the floors.
_____ I wash the windows.
_____ I wash the walls.
_____ I junk my junk.

BED
_____ I make my own bed.
_____ I make the children's or guest beds.
_____ I change the sheets.

BATH
_____ I hang up my wet towel after I shower or bathe.
_____ I wipe down the shower walls or wipe out the bath.
_____ I clean my beard or mustache trimmings out of the sink.
_____ I clean the toilet.

FOOD
_____I help plan meals.
_____I shop for groceries and put them away.
_____I cook meals.
_____I do the dishes and put them away.
_____I clean out the refrigerator and defrost the freezer.
_____I take out the garbage.

LAUNDRY
_____I hang up my clothes if they're clean enough to wear again.
_____I put my dirty clothes in the laundry basket.
_____I do the washing.
_____I do the drying.
_____I iron my own shirts.

CHILDREN (if single or have no children, score a 2 for each.)
_____I help out with the school projects.
_____I nurse them or take them to the doctor when they're sick.
_____I take them shopping for clothes.
_____I change their diapers and help with potty training.

One thing to note is that Aslett's quiz does not take into account other chores around the house, such as household and mechanical repairs and yard work. In making a final determination of whether your husband is pulling his share of the load, these factors should be considered.

2. Divide the labor equally. Patricia Gundry, in *Heirs Together*, suggested that couples list the broad areas of work responsibility, then determine who has the most competence or interest in each area. Next they should determine if the person wants the job or would like to share it. She suggested that if one person had skills in a particular area, he or she might want to train the other to do that function. She also stressed the importance of sharing things fairly.[15]

The overall purpose of this procedure is to come up with a series of mini-contracts—agreements that will bring mutual satisfaction. These contracts do not have to be set in stone; they can be renegotiated as people and circumstances change. But it is important before taking on a new responsibility to carefully consider the impact of the change being made. It is also important to allow time for the agreements to work successfully. Don't short-circuit the process by jumping in when your mate doesn't seem to be following through as you want him to.

For example, Joanna and Greg had an agreement to take turns getting up in the middle of the night when their infant woke up crying. One evening, when the baby woke up, Greg continued snoring. Joanna gently woke him up. Greg acted very irritated and stomped his way to the baby's room. Joanna started to feel guilty and then angry at Greg (after all, it was *his* turn). She realized what she was doing and decided to let Greg be angry without reacting to him, and she went back to sleep. The next morning everything was normal. Greg was just upset about having to get up; he wasn't really angry at Joanna.

3. Together, establish specific time periods when he is solely responsible for the kids (such as bathtime or storytime). Work toward making it a ritual that takes place regularly at the appointed hour.

"Let our husbands share in child care as much as possible," advised Patricia Gundry in *Heirs Together*. She related a story told to her by a woman she had met at a student wives' meeting. The woman said, "When our children were small, I tried to free my husband as much as I could from home duties so he could do his work unhindered. I wouldn't do that again if I had it to do over. I think I denied him some of the pleasures of caring for his children, getting to know all those things mothers are there to see."[16]

4. At first, while your husband is still adjusting, it's not helpful to be too critical. There's no better way to discourage a man's participation than to criticize his work. His typical response will be, "Then why don't you just do it yourself?"

A better response is to show appreciation. Say things like, "Hey, honey, thanks for cleaning the kitchen. It made me feel so good to get up this morning to a clean kitchen. You're wonderful." That's called positive reinforcement.

5. Be flexible and negotiate as necessary. There are times when one of you will not be able to carry through. Accept that. Don't keep score, but be ready to negotiate alternative plans. Compromise is often needed.

6. Recognize that equitable workloads may not be equal. Take Roger and Mary, for example. She's willing to iron his shirts

if he'll take care of her car. He washes it, maintains it, and fills it with gas for her, which takes an average of one hour per week. Mary, on the other hand, spends just under two hours ironing his shirts every week—but she considers this fair exchange. She'd rather spend an extra hour ironing every week than have to fill her gas tank when it's cold and rainy. Let's face it. Some tasks are more unpleasant than others. So take that into consideration, and reward each other for harsh duty.

7. Learn to relax. Look at the big picture. Does it really matter whether your floors shine or your pans sparkle? Or does it hurt to sleep on dirty sheets? The dirt will still be there tomorrow. We've heard more than one mother say that she wishes she had put aside her chores for a while and played house or hide-and-go-seek with her kids. Now they're all grown up with families of their own. The laughter's gone—and there's no way to bring it back.

8. Get away by yourself once in a while and let Dad take over. Most men don't fully appreciate all the things their wives do until the wives aren't around. Nor do they learn how to manage the kids, cook, or do laundry until they have no choice. That's why many women have found that just a little bit of traveling on the job can do wonders for resolving the partnership crisis. By just getting away for an afternoon, you can help sharpen his skills and heighten his awareness.

If you are to have transformed relationships, it is important to break free of anyone else's ideas about how you should live your marriage. We tend to adopt a variety of models, ranging from our parents' marriage to other people's ideas, but it is healthier for couples to determine for themselves how they wish to structure their relationship.

Role prescriptions do not take our individuality into account. What if a man enjoys domestic chores and his wife likes to tinker on cars? Should we restrict their outlets because they are deviating from the norm? One woman related to Tim that she was frustrated because she liked to work on cars (she had learned how to change the oil and plugs from her father), but her husband didn't want her to work on the family car.

Many partnerships between good friends who decide to do business together go down the tubes because they assume that the friendship will transcend any difficulties that may arise. It is the same in a marriage. We hope love will conquer all, but when you get down to the nitty-gritty of who's going to change the diapers, many couples don't survive the conflict. A good marriage is well defined, and communication is instrumental to the defining process.

The adjustments and transitions that we've discussed are big steps. Perhaps you are satisfied with well-defined patterns that you have lived with for years—i.e., "This is *my* kitchen, thank you," or "The garage is *his* domain, and that's just the way it is." If so—great. But if you feel change is necessary, the steps we've given can be a helpful path toward transformation.

CONCLUSION

*Y*ou may be thinking that happy, fulfilling relationships are beyond your reach. The transformation we've suggested in this book may seem like an impossible dream. But it is not. Step by step, there are ways for you to begin on a path that can take you where you want to be in your relationship. Yes, it may involve risk, pain, and hard work. Risk because under the stress of change, some relationships might get worse before they get better. Pain because old patterns are painful to change. Hard work because it takes unceasing effort to break out of the old and stay on the path toward the new.

But ultimately we tend to become the people *we* choose to be. In a sense, although we live together in relationships, we tend to *grow* alone. The resolve and effort we are willing to extract from ourselves determine the results we will realize in our relationships.

There is hope. There is rarely any circumstance that cannot be better, any person who cannot change, any relationship that cannot improve. Occasionally, however, a couple gets locked into destructive patterns, and regardless of how they try to get out, they spin their wheels deeper. This is when outside counseling can bring new insights and objectivity. If this is where you are, consider going to a counselor (pastor or therapist), checking in advance for good references. Don't feel defeated by your seeking counsel; it is a *courageous* choice.

Above all, remember your ultimate Source—Jesus Christ. He offers hope for every individual and can give the strength that we need. All of us are flawed. But if our focus is right, we can "lay aside every weight, and the sin which so easily ensnares us, and . . . run with endurance the race that is set before us, looking unto Jesus, the author and finisher of our faith" (Heb. 2:1–2).

Notes

CHAPTER 1

1. Romans 12:1.
2. Warren Farrell, *Why Men Are the Way They Are: The Male-Female Dynamic* (New York: McGraw-Hill, 1986), 115.
3. Ibid., 117.
4. Ibid., 121.
5. Ibid., 124.
6. Ibid., 134.
7. Karen Shanor, *The Shanor Study: The Sexual Sensitivity of the American Male* (New York: Dial, 1978), 253.
8. Farrell, *Why Men Are*, 56.
9. Anne Wilson Schaef, *Women's Reality: An Emerging Female System in the White Male Society* (Minneapolis, MN: Winston, 1981), 2.
10. Ibid., 8–9.
11. Ibid., 9.
12. Ibid., 11.
13. Ibid., 28.
14. Ibid., 29.
15. Ibid., 29–32.
16. Farrell, *Why Men Are*, 56.
17. Alice Rossi, quoted in Joyce Brothers, *What Every Woman Should Know about Men* (New York: Ballentine, 1985).

CHAPTER 2.

1. Brothers, *What Every Woman Should Know,* 15.
2. Ibid., 13.
3. Ibid., 19.
4. Ibid.
5. "A User's Guide to Hormones," *Newsweek,* Jan. 12, 1987, 50.
6. Brothers, 53.
7. Joyce Brothers, *The Brothers System for Liberated Love and Marriage* (New York: Avon, 1973), 192.
8. Helen Block Lewis, *Psychic War in Men and Women* (New York: Univ. Press, 1976), 47.
9. Walter Trobisch, *The Misunderstood Man* (Downer's Grove, IL: InterVarsity, 1983), 31.
10. Brothers, *The Brothers System,* 22.

11. Ibid.
12. Ibid., 23.
13. Ibid., 22.
14. Ibid., 25.
15. Ibid., 24.
16. Ibid., 31.
17. Ibid.
18. Doreen Kimura, "Male Brain, Female Brain: The Hidden Difference," *Psychology Today,* Nov. 1985, 56.
19. Psalm 139:14.

CHAPTER 3

1. Gilbert Bilezikian, *Beyond Sex Roles: A Guide for the Study of Female Roles in the Bible* (Grand Rapids, MI: Baker Book House, 1985), 25.
2. Donald M. Joy, *Bonding: Relationships in the Image of God* (Waco, TX: Word, 1985), 16.
3. Bilezikian, *Beyond Sex Roles,* 50.
4. Joy, *Bonding,* 17.
5. Ibid., 25.

CHAPTER 4

1. Martin Acker, "Real Men," *Old Oregon,* Wtr. 1986, 28–30.
2. Marcia Gutentag and Susan Salasin, "Women/Men and Mental Health," presented at the Aspen Conference on Women, 1975.
3. M. Simner, "Newborn Response to the Cry of Another Infant," *Developmental Psychology,* 5 (1971), 136–150.
4. Rubin, Provenzano, Luria, "The Eye of the Beholder: Parents' View on Sex of Newborns," *American Journal of Orthopsychiatry,* 44 (1974), 512–519.
5. Moss, "Sex, Age and State Determinants of Mother-Infant Interaction," *Merrel–Palmer Quarterly,* 13 (1967), 19–36.
6. Robson, Pederson, Moss, "Developmental Observations of Dyadic Gazing in Relation to Fear of Strangers and Social Approach Behavior," *Child Development,* 40 (1969), 619–627.
7. Goldberg and Lewis, "Play Behavior in the Year Old Infant: Early Sex Differences," *Child Development,* 40 (1969), 21–32.
8. Carol Gilligan, *In a Different Voice* (Cambridge, MA: Harvard Univ. Press, 1981), 10.
9. Adams, "Adolescent Personal Problems as a Function of Age and Sex," *Journal of Genetic Psychology,* 104 (1964), 207–214.
10. Gilligan, *In a Different Voice,* 10.
11. Ibid., 8.
12. Bernie Zilbergeld and John Ullman, *Male Sexuality: A Guide to Sexual Fulfillment* (Denver: Little, 1978).

CHAPTER 5

1. John Powell, *The Secret of Staying in Love* (Valencia, CA: Argus Communications, 1974), 11–12.

2. Goldberg, "Are Men Prejudiced Against Women?" *Transaction,* May 1968, 28–30.
3. Crandall, Preston, and Katkowsky, "Motivational and Ability Determinants of Young Children's Intellectual Achievement Behaviors," *Child Development,* 33 (1962), 642–61.
4. Carol Tavris with Dr. Alice Baumgartner, "How Would Your Life Be Different If You'd Been Born a Boy?" *Redbook,* Feb. 1983, 92–95.
5. Matteson, *Adolescence Today: Sex Roles and the Search for Identity,* Dorsey Press, 1975.
6. Trobisch, *The Misunderstood Man,* 18.
7. Ibid., 21.
8. Marc Fasteau, *The Male Machine* (New York: Dell, 1976).
9. Matteson, *Adolescence Today,* 84.

CHAPTER 6

1. Joy, *Bonding,* 25.
2. Schaef, *Women's Reality,* 108.
3. Ibid., 109.
4. Pierre Mornell, *Passive Men, Wild Women* (New York: Simon and Schuster, 1979), 24.
5. Farrell, *Why Men Are,* 166.
6. Lee Benham and Alexandra Benham, "Employment, Earning and Psychiatric Diagnosis," in *Economic Aspects of Health,* ed. Victor Fuchs (Chicago: Univ. of Chicago Press, 1982), 203–220.
7. Farrell, *Why Men Are,* 150.
8. Ibid., 150.
9. Schaef, *Women's Reality,* 54–55.
10. Larson and Knapp, "Sex Differences in Symbolic Conceptions of the Deity," *Journal of Projective Techniques and Personality Assessment* (1968–69), 303–306.

CHAPTER 7

1. Gilda Berger, *Women, Work and Wages* (New York: Franklin Watts, 1986), 24.
2. Ibid., 25.
3. Susan Brownmiller, *Femininity* (New York: Linden, 1984), 49.
4. Page Smith, *Daughters of the Promised Land* (New York: Little Brown, 1970), 317.
5. M. Scott Peck, *The Road Less Traveled* (New York: Simon and Schuster, 1978), 166.
6. Lewis Smedes, presentation to Conference of Evangelical Christian Publishers Association, Palm Springs, CA, Jan. 13, 1986.
7. Albert Ellis and Robert A. Harper, *A New Guide to Rational Living* (North Hollywood, CA: Wilshire Book Co., 1975).

CHAPTER 8

1. William J. Diehm, "Building Self-Esteem," *Today's Christian Woman,* Summer 1983, 108.

2. Bruce Narramore, *You're Somebody Special* (Grand Rapids, MI: Zondervan, 1978).

CHAPTER 9

1. C. S. Lewis, *The Screwtape Letters* (New York: Macmillan, 1982), 52.
2. Sandra Simpson LeSourd, *The Compulsive Woman* (Old Tappan, NJ: Revell, Chosen Books, 1987), 1–2.
3. Peck, *The Road*, 99.
4. Ibid., 108.
5. Maggie Scarf, *Unfinished Business*, 568–69.
6. Cathy Guisewite, "Cathy," *The Equal Rights Monitor*, May-June 1977, 5.
7. Dietrich Bonhoeffer, *Life Together* (New York: Harper & Row, 1976), 36.
8. John Powell, *The Secret of Staying in Love* (Valencia, CA: Tabor Publishing, 1974), 54.
9. Ibid., 22.

CHAPTER 10

1. Peck, *The Road*, 97.

CHAPTER 11

1. Anne Atkins, *Split Image: Male and Female after God's Likeness* (Grand Rapids, MI: Eerdman's, 1987), 59.
2. Ibid., 56–58.
3. Ibid., 58–59.
4. Kari Torgese Malcolm, *Women at the Crossroads: A Path Beyond Feminism and Traditionalism* (Downers Grove, IL: InterVarsity Press, 1982), 80–81.
5. Ibid.
6. Bilezikian, *Beyond Sex Roles*, 158.
7. C. S. Lewis, *The Four Loves* (London: Peter Smith, 1960), 199–121.
8. Brothers, *The Brothers System*, 119.

CHAPTER 12

1. Bonhoeffer, *Life Together*, 35–36.

CHAPTER 13

1. Ruth Senter, *The Seasons of Friendship* (Grand Rapids: Zondervan, 1982).
2. Paul Tournier, *The Gift of Feeling* (Atlanta: John Knox Press, 1981), 63.

CHAPTER 14

1. Naifeh and Smith, *Why Can't Men Open Up?*, 134.
2. George R. Bach and Peter Wyden, *The Intimate Enemy: How to Fight Fair in Love and Marriage* (New York: Avon, 1968).
3. Quoted in Naifeh and Smith, *Why Can't Men Open Up?* 99–100.

CHAPTER 15

1. Peter Marin, "A Revolution's Broken Promises," *Psychology Today*, July 1982, 54.
2. Ibid., 54.

3. Ibid., 54.
4. Lois L. Davitz and Joel Davitz, *Living in Sync: Men and Women in Love* (New York: Bergh Publishers, 1986), 83.
5. Ibid., 83.
6. Ibid., 84.

CHAPTER 16

1. "Marriage: What Women Expect and What They Get," *McCall's*.
2. "Yuppie Love: The Sex Life of the Two-Career Couple," *Working Woman Magazine*, Aug. 1984, 102.
3. Allen Bloom, *The Closing of the American Mind* (New York: Simon and Schuster, 1987), 129.
4. Ibid., 130.
5. Ibid.
6. Ibid., 131.
7. Ibid.
8. Ibid.
9. David Viscott, *How to Live with Another Person* (New York: Pocket Books, 1974), 31.
10. "Housework, His/Hers and Hers," *Bend Bulletin*, Aug. 9, 1987, D1.
11. Brothers, *What Every Woman Should Know,* 257.
12. "Housework, His/Hers and Hers," D1.
13. Naifeh and Smith, *Why Can't Men Open Up?*, 40.
14. Don Aslett, "Quiz: In Search of Macho Men," *Bend Bulletin*, Sept. 10, 1987.
15. Gundry, *Heirs Together,* 132.
16. Ibid., 138–142.